Bill Barnes
11/13/01

HOPE FOR THE WORLD

HOPE FOR THE WORLD

Mission in a Global Context

Papers from the Campbell Seminar

EDITED BY WALTER BRUEGGEMANN

Westminster John Knox Press
LOUISVILLE
LONDON • LEIDEN

© 2001 by Westminster John Knox Press

Scripture quotations from the New Revised Standard Version of the Bible are copyright © 1989 by the Division of Christian Education of the National Council of the Churches of Christ in the U.S.A. and are used by permission.

Book design by Sharon Adams
Cover design by Cynthia Dunne
Cover art: Comstock

First edition
Published by Westminster John Knox Press
Louisville, Kentucky

This book is printed on acid-free paper that meets the American National Standards Institute Z39.48 standard. ∞

PRINTED IN THE UNITED STATES OF AMERICA

01 02 03 04 05 06 07 08 09 10–10 9 8 7 6 5 4 3 2 1

Library of Congress Cataloging-in-Publication Data

Campbell Seminar (2000 : Columbia Theological Seminary)
    Hope for the world : mission in a global context : papers from the Campbell Seminar / edited by Walter Brueggemann.
        p. cm.
    Includes bibliographical references and index.
    ISBN 0-664-22461-X (alk. paper)
    1. Missions—Congresses. I. Brueggemann, Walter. II. Title.

BV2020 .C36 2001
266'.009'051—dc21
                                                                                2001026339

Contents

Part One

Introduction

Chapter One

Missional Questions in a Fresh Context

Walter Brueggemann

The Theme: Mission as Hope in Action

Columbia Theological Seminary has had, for a long time, a serious, active commitment to providing an international dimension in its curricular program. This has been most visibly expressed through the MDiv Alternative Context Program that has, for many years, been a central focus of faculty commitment of time, money, and energy. More recently, the same accent on "alternative context" has been extended to the DMin curriculum. These programs receive a great deal of student attention and evidently generate a good deal of fresh awareness and critical theological reflection on our campus.

This volume is a report on the launch of a wholly new effort around a commitment to international accents in theological education at Columbia. The seminary has received an immensely generous legacy from John Bulow Campbell, the seminary's major donor, through the Campbell Foundation. Largely through the imagination of my colleague, Erskine Clarke, the faculty has initiated what will be an annual seminar, the Campbell Seminar, the first session of which convened on campus, September 18–November 10, 2000. The seminar was constituted by five international church leaders, two Presbyterian pastors who are graduates of the seminary, and one seminary faculty member (for a roster, see Appendix A). The seminar was designed so that its members could be free of other professional obligations and devote full time to the interaction of its members for eight weeks, and for the most part that full-time commitment has prevailed among the members of the seminar.

At the outset, the faculty provided a general prospectus to clarify a theme for the seminar, "Mission as Hope in Action." (See Appendix B). It will be evident in what follows in this book that the members of the seminar stayed close to the theme proposed by the faculty and found the faculty prospectus an important and generative question. There was, moreover, a general but unspecified expectation on the part of the faculty of a written outcome from the work of the seminar, this book fulfilling that expectation. Between the initial faculty prospectus and the general anticipation of a written outcome, the seminar was completely free to order its own life and determine its own procedures for its work. I am glad to report that the seminar formed, jelled, and conducted its work in an alert, intense, sustained, and generative way—I suggest, well beyond what any of us might have dared to hope in advance.

Two by-products of the seminar may be mentioned. First, because members of the seminar were full-time residents on campus, they were able to engage informally in a variety of rich ways with students and faculty members, much to the benefit of the seminary community. The presence of this group of pastors and scholars has had an immense effect upon the life and horizon of the seminary. Contacts have included chapel leadership, forum presentations, participation in a number of classes, formal faculty input in the seminar, and endless conversations in the dining hall, plus hospitality extended by faculty in a variety of ways.

Second, the several members of the seminar in their home contexts carry exceptionally heavy leadership responsibilities in their own church settings, as pastors, teachers, and administrators. Indeed, they are characteristically overextended and endlessly give of their lives generously and without reservation. For that reason, the seminar has been an important sabbatical break for its members. Even though our time together in the seminar has been intense and demanding, there has also been a treasured opportunity for sabbatic rest, reflection, and research. In this modest and indirect way, I have no doubt that the seminary, through the seminar, has contributed to the well-being of the church in contexts other than and very different from its own.

The Working of the Seminar

The work of the seminar, structured in a collegial way by the members themselves, has eventuated in four waves of discussion, research, and writing, three of which are reflected in the present volume.

First, we took considerable time at the outset to *introduce ourselves* to each other, because we were, for the most part, strangers to one another. Members of the seminar chose to introduce themselves variously. Invariably, these narrative introductions were deeply contextual and intimately concrete. These introductory narratives were consistently a ready self-disclosure that contributed immediately to our becoming a serious collegium of critical reflection, prepared to make personal histories important resources and reference points for what was to follow. The personal narrative process reminded us that in the end the missional reality of the church is given in this way, not first of all as impersonal institutional form, as it may sometimes appear, given our usual ways of "church history." Nor is the missional reality of the church expressed primally in erudite intellectual articulation. Important as institutional form and intellectual expression are to the faithful mission of the church, behind and before these are real persons who have been named and claimed by the gospel through communities of praise and obedience. These claimed members think, imagine, and act in attentive ways, and that thought, imagination, and action often have import completely disproportionate to its intended scope. Our first engagement was to discover afresh this concreteness of the church.

Second, another round of introductions—which took even longer and required much more psychic energy—was *reflection on our concrete sociohistorical, ecclesial contexts*. (This round of introductions is presented in this volume as "context papers.") In hearing these presentations and now in rereading them, I am struck by the concrete particularity of each personal presentation of context. The local markings that matter decisively for the telling of context turn on specific details and nameable crisis events that are most often not even reported to "the outside" and, if reported, seldom noticed or remembered by "outsiders." Moreover, I am immediately moved by and made aware of the way in which each member of the seminar lives in a revolutionary circumstance, a revolution in some places more dramatic than in others, and in some places more positive and hopeful than in others.

As I have heard these several deeply moving context-disclosures, I am impressed by the way in which recent historical developments in every place represented in our conversation are marked, characteristically, by the deep and defining tension between "the big ones" and "the little ones." That tension is regularly shaped by unbearable incongruities issuing in cynicism and violence, on the one hand, and by steadfast courage and visions of freedom on the other hand. Regularly, the reports on socioecclesial contexts have turned not only on how the force of state power or corporate power tends to run roughshod over human fragility but also on the strange resurgences of human possibility through which the power of the Spirit surfaces and surfaces again in defiance and resolve, in freedom, and in obedience to what God intends.

Third, members of the seminar were, for good reason, insistent on the specificity and concreteness of the missional question in local circumstance. That insistence, moreover, proved to be a crucial reference point, a major source of energy, and perhaps our deepest strength in a conversation that we found to be Spirit-led. Quite clearly and perhaps not surprisingly, the local reference points for understanding and deciding about mission proved at the end, as at the beginning, to be quite incommensurate with each other.

For that reason, it is all the more astonishing that, given such local histories of hurt and such local, God-given options for the future, we were able to sense together, early in our conversation, our *common convictions* that issued in what we have referred to as our "consensus paper." (See chapter 2.) Through a series of outlines, drafts, critiques, edits, and new drafts, we arrived rather early at the main theses that became that document. I do not wish to overstate or overdramatize the emergence of the consensus points. But I believe that all members of the seminar will long remember the moment when Douglas John Hall, our scribe in this matter, read what became the governing draft for that paper. Hearing it was a sober moment for us, for each of us readily recognized the allusions to earlier discussion and the references to our local insistences and phrasings, but we also were aware in that moment of hearing that each of us had moved and all of us had moved together into awarenesses and convictions where none of us had begun.

When the the later draft was read, there was a pause among us and then a rising applause, as we sensed together that we had been led as a genuine community to a new place. I do not want to claim too much for our consensus paper. Indeed, to some of our readers, the statement may seem commonplace. But as is always the case in such a venture, part of the reality of the outcome is the process of getting there, a process by which we have been led beyond ourselves to a common statement to which we can all gladly assent.

At the same time, I do not want to overstate the importance of "getting there," important as that has been to those of us in the collegium. What will count for our readers is the statement that we offer here. Among the important accents to which we have been led together, beyond where any of us would have arrived alone, are these convictions:

- That the world church, in all its parts, faces a new context for ministry and an opportunity for mission, a context marked by a despair commonly shared by "haves" and "have-nots," even if a failure of hope marks and assaults different communities in different circumstances very differently.
- That this new situation of despair, deeply rooted in spiritual crisis, manifests itself economically, politically, and militarily in the new globalization of wealth that admits of immense concentrations of power and wealth and, commensurately, immense deficiencies and deprivations.
- That the old patterns of European and, more recently, U.S. domination—in state, in economy, and in church—are everywhere important for defining and discerning the common, varied contexts of despair.
- That the old notions of "mission" are deeply saturated with ideologies of domination, so that we may sense a congruity between older triumphalist notions of mission and newer modes of globalization, from both of which there is urgent cause for repentance and emancipation.
- That hope as an evangelical antidote to despair cannot be practiced triumphally but requires an ecclesial sense of vulnerability, formed by the truth of the cross as an ecclesial marking.
- That pluralism positions the church (with its narrative of hope) without an absolute claim that is inherently triumphalist; rather, the church is entrusted with a readiness for allies in hope among other believers and among those of good will who stand outside every "believing community."
- That the church, with the important gains and sorry distortions of Christendom, must in the future practice its mission of "telling inside" and "enacting outside" with a due sense of humility. That humility is rooted in an awareness that distinguishes between its own mission as a gift of God and the

mission of God that takes place not only in and through the church's mission but also before, outside, alongside the church's best obedience, and against the church when it is disobedient.

It is clear to us in the seminar that these several convictions, more fully explicated in our consensus paper, reflect a huge imperative and an equally large invitation for the church to rethink and reimagine its own life as a missional force responsive to our Risen Lord and congruent with that Risen Lord in his passion and suffering.

In the fourth wave, upon agreement about the consensus paper, members of the seminar wrote *expository papers* around the main theses of the consensus paper, to give more personal elaboration to a particular theme and to have the liberty of understanding and presenting that theme with particular contextual reference. (See part three.) These papers received careful scrutiny through discussion in the seminar; in the end, however, these are personal papers, and each writer was completely free to make a statement in the context of our common work without the assent of other members of the seminar.

Because the seminar included three U.S. persons attached to the seminary as graduates and as faculty, and because the seminar identified the shape of the missional crisis with reference to U.S. domination—economic, political, and ecclesial—it was the issue of U.S. state and economic imperialism that especially occupied us in the latter days of our seminar. It is fair to say that the internationals in our seminar felt strongly that the crisis in the church's mission is reflective of the centrality and domination in the world economies. It is equally fair to say that U.S. persons in the seminar did not easily and readily accept, without nuance, such a harsh verdict. The matter continued to occupy us in a good spirit of friendliness; that it occupied us, however, indicates the deep force of the critique and the urgent attention it must receive in the U.S. church.

The church in the United States is, of course, called to a vocation and mission that puts it in tension with the realities of U.S. political, economic, and military power. Sometimes the U.S. church is deeply implicated in these public realities. And very often the U.S. church has acted according to its distinctive calling in Christ as a force for transformative good. Although the U.S. church is often in an ambiguous place and acts as a mixed blessing, members of the seminar celebrate the generosity and compassion of the U.S. church that are enacted quite concretely in the world church. In any case, the truth of the gospel of the cross poses deep challenges for the U.S. church, challenges that have immediate and concrete force among us.

Continued Reverberations

I turn to a reflection on the Campbell Seminar and its effect among us. No one in the planning process for the seminar could have foreseen the deep and positive impact that the seminar has had and will continue to have in the seminary community. Partly that impact is because we at the seminary (and, more generally, the U.S. church) live at a critical turning point in our thinking about the gospel; the question of mission is just now enormously germane to our common life. It is clear from any critical reflection that old missional assumptions and practices are no longer credible or productive, but the way ahead is not yet clear. The reality of religious pluralism, moreover, requires that mission be reformulated to recognize that God's mission is much larger than the horizon of the church and that consequently the church's mission cannot be conceived or practiced in absolutist or triumphalist terms. Recognition of the larger scope of God's mission and acceptance of a nontriumphalist posture for the church mission, moreover, may free the church for a generous agency in the world as a hope-bearing, hope-generating servant people.

Another reason that the seminar will have such impact on the seminary over time is a factor that we could not have imagined ahead of time, the self-giving generosity of the members of the seminar. Every one of them has given boundlessly to the life of the school, has been available, thoughtful, and receptive in every way possible. Indeed, the way in which the members of the seminar have been present surely is a model for how interchurch hospitality works at its best.

The first constituency that the seminar intends to address is, of course, the community of Columbia Theological Seminary. The seminary has initiated the seminar not only because of a formal commitment to an international dimension or program but also because it hopes and expects that the seminar will provide input to the seminary as Columbia moves into a new phase of its life under a new president. My judgment is that the output of the seminar provides for the seminary a rich offer of materials and resources for rethinking the contours of its mission for the days ahead.

The seminary is marked (a) by a long history of occupying "a middle way" on every question, (b) by living in a richly religious South with a vibrant Presbyterian constituency, and (c) by an environment of immense institutional affluence. In that context, the redefinition of the mission of the church as a hope-generating servant community open to many allies is an important opportunity. I suspect that the invitation for rethinking and repositioning may touch every part of the life of the seminary, but most immediately and directly it concerns the faculty as it considers pedagogical and curricular issues. It is my judgment that curricular questions become less urgent and less important while "underneath questions" of *context and mission* take on greater importance, for the matters of context and mission are likely to be defining, no matter what shape the curriculum takes.

In the initiation of this seminar, Columbia Theological Seminary may offer to other seminaries and theological schools an important model for future educational work. So far as I know, this particular kind of seminar, focused on sustained international and pastoral input into a particular U.S. seminary context, is without parallel. Such an undertaking requires immense energy and generous financial resources. I have no doubt, nonetheless, that the seminar, in its cumulative effect over a period of years, will be a defining factor in the future of the seminary, a defining factor well worth what it cost in terms of time, energy, and money. It is inevitable that a seminary will, when it can, settle into the routines of domesticated issues that are congruent with a church constituency that is itself not overly eager for change. In such a settled, conventional context, to have an ongoing conversation that includes respected, authoritative voices other than our own is profoundly important. It is the voice of the neighbor from another context who bears inescapable witness that we are not our own.

The seminary will be, in continually reverberating ways, the recipient of the witness of the seminar. Beyond that, of course, the seminary exists for the church its serves. Thus the long-term effect of the seminar may be upon the church in its congregational articulation. It is clear that the force of secularism and the challenge of pluralism prove that Christian congregations in the United States—even in the most stable religious environment of the South—cannot continue for long in old patterns. It is possible to view that emerging reality as a threat that should receive a defensive response. It is plausible, however, that what feels like threat to old patterns may be, in fact, a God-given opportunity for local congregations to reembrace God-given vocation. Imagine:

- A congregation with a limited-scope but deeply embraced mission, not needing to be God's sole agent in the neighborhood.
- A congregation with a clear gospel, but open to allies, not needing to be a lone presence in the community.
- A congregation saturated with Easter-rooted hope, offering an alternative to communities of fear, anger, and greed, an alternative given in vulnerability and generosity.

Imagine! These, of course, are not new marks for the church, for in some ways the church has always enacted these wonders. But at a point of such serious disengagement to which the church is greatly tempted (for which internal rage in the church is a sign and symptom), the trajectory of faith and ministry from the seminar may be an occasion for head-clearing, faith-embracing, new resolve. Not everything is entrusted to a local congregation. But that hope by the Spirit is given in, with, and under congregational life is a wonder of God that creates new futures.

It is possible to imagine that the seminar will have a durable ripple effect among us. It is not unimportant that the saint most often cited in the seminar by a number of members was Dietrich Bonhoeffer. Bonhoeffer, of course, produced a number of stunning aphorisms that are pertinent to us. His witness leaves us nothing greater than the assurance that a life of obedience is a way to freedom enacted as hope. That good word, so well exposited in the seminar, is a powerful invitation for fresh mission.

It remains for me to express thanks in two directions. First, we at Columbia Theological Seminary are deeply indebted to the members of the seminar. It is no small matter to be away from home in a giving posture for eight weeks, but it was so for the members of the seminar. The way in which these colleagues have entered into the work of the seminar and the life of the seminary is a rare gift to us all. Second, thanks are due colleagues of faculty and staff for the attentive practices of hospitality to our guests. Specifically, thanks are due Dean Erskine Clarke for his deep vision for internationalism in our program and for his daily, sustained commitment to the project; thanks are offered to Bonnie Shoemaker, who did much of the heavy lifting that made the seminar viable; finally, thanks are expressed to Bobby Williamson, who attended to details for the seminar in helpful ways.

In his great ethical invitation, Paul urges the church in Rome: Extend hospitality to strangers (Romans 12:13).

The seminary is a hospitable place, and it has welcomed these strangers, who have turned out to be companions in faith and in wonderment. But finally the measure of hospitality is our capacity to receive, welcome, and host new thinking and new obedience that constitute both a judgment on what has been among us and a gift of hope for what can yet be. The measure of hospitality that receives newness in strange forms, as the consensus paper says about another matter, will be determined "day by day, year by year, decade by decade." The seminar will address us for many days and many years and many decades, but the first day of the first year of the first decade for rethinking in hope is upon us this day.

The work of the seminar has made it clear that hope, if it is grounded in the gospel, must be concrete, embodied, and context specific. Among other things, that quality of hope includes language that is concrete and context specific. As a consequence, this book permits each member of the seminar to speak in a voice that is peculiar and particular and historically rooted. I have not tried to edit out such voices but believe that respecting and retaining such voices is appropriate to our purpose. The reader may therefore occasionally find rhetoric that is jarring or rough in terms of conventions of Western academic rhetoric. Our seminar was not constituted by "Western academics," but by passionate Christians who are academically competent and who care most about the concrete church. Thus our varied modes of articulation pertain to the very faith we confess and to the very mission we affirm.

Chapter Two

Hope from Old Sources for a New Century

A Consensus Paper

This chapter presents the summation of the work of the Campbell Seminar to which all of its members could assent. We have retained the form of an address to our host institution, Columbia Theological Seminary. It is a primal hope of the seminary, as well as the members of the seminar, that the paper will become a defining reference point for future work of the seminary. It is presented here because the members of the seminar believe that our common statement has important resonance well beyond the seminar. Thus, we are glad to have a wider circle of readers attend to our argument. It is our hope that this statement not only defines in a sharper way "the mission field" but also addresses the matter of how the effort as "mission" might be shaped differently. Thus, the address to the seminary should reach beyond the seminary as well, to all who face these demanding issues. We believe that the rubric of despair-hope is pertinent to the new questions now facing the church and that this articulation warrants careful attention.

To the Students, Teachers, Officers, and Board of ColumbiaTheological Seminary, and to All Who Strive for Faithfulness to Jesus Christ at a Time of Change and Uncertainty

Grace to you, and peace:

We are eight persons, representative of several provinces of the ecumenical church, whom you have called together to contemplate the mission of the Christian church in the century just begun. We are sincerely grateful for the foresight, trust, and generosity that you have shown in making it possible for us to enter into a wonderfully sustained and deeply meaningful conversation on a subject of vital importance to us all. Each of us would testify that we have not only been enriched but also been changed in significant ways, through this unusual opportunity and experience.

There has emerged, besides, an exceptionally high degree of unanimity in the thought and discourse that we have shared over these eight weeks. Both in our discernment of the times through which we are passing and in our approach to the church's calling in such times, we have found ourselves again and again voicing the same or very similar points of view. Though we do indeed represent continental contexts that differ from one another significantly (Latin America, Asia, Europe, Africa, and North America) and though our theological emphases vary, sometimes, on that account, we have experienced such a bond of Christian mutuality and understanding that it is our wish to attempt, now, a common statement, in which to convey to you concretely both the urgency we feel for a renewed theology and practice of Christian mission and the possibilities that we sense for its enactment.

This brief statement cannot, of course, do justice to all aspects of the topic. At many points, it will beg questions and leave assumptions unspecified. Throughout, elaboration will be minimal. For that reason, we are submitting together with our common statement sixteen supplementary essays, written by the individual members of the seminar. These essays, in earlier forms, preceded the composition of the common statement and are, in large measure, the background of reflection and discussion out of which the latter was penned. Although the supplementary essays represent the unimpeded work of their individual authors, they nonetheless achieved, in their presentation to the seminar at large, nearly universal approbation. We therefore commend them to you as an integral aspect of our *common* work.

The Mission of the Christian Movement in the Twenty-First Century Is to Confess Hope in Action

Christianity Has Entered a New Phase

Unevenly but decisively, the long sojourn of the Christian religion as the established cultus of the Western world has almost spent itself. Although pockets of "Christendom" persist, and the temptation to religious hegemony and triumphalism is perennial, the process of Christian disestablishment seems likely to continue throughout the present century and beyond. Increasingly in all lands, Christian faith will become a matter of decision, taken in the face of many obstacles and alternatives and sustained by disciplined thought, prayer, and the support of the *koinonia*. The Holy Spirit and not the *esprit* of an allegedly Christian society is already, and will increasingly be known to be, the generative Source of life and faith in the post-Christendom church.

Mission, under these circumstances, must be profoundly reconsidered. Christians may no longer entertain the "Christianization" of the world as a faithful expression of Christ's mandate. While Christian missionary endeavor has often been well intentioned and beneficial to countless human beings, it has seldom been free of ambiguity. During the past century, sensitive Christians have had to ponder the violence that has so frequently accompanied Christendom's attempts to "win the world for Christ," including the subtle deprecation of the cults and cultures of other peoples. In view of today's conspicuously pluralistic and fragile global context, an aggressive missionary zeal on the part of Christians only contributes to the further fragmentation of planetary life.

This realization has brought about much confusion in Christian bodies that, a century ago, had embraced policies of worldwide mission and hoped to see the twentieth century become "the Christian century." Some contemporary Christians deplore any talk of mission at all. Such confusion may prove salutary, for, clearly, there is no *easy* way of moving from Christendom to the future church. Perhaps for centuries still, Christianity, especially in its Western expression, will cast the shadow of an imperial religion that, its message of love and reconciliation notwithstanding, imposed its religious and cultural assumptions upon others. Especially where Christianity has been dominant and militant, Christians must now be prepared to listen, to wait, and to serve. Christian stewardship of life through the pursuit of justice, peace, and the well-being of creation will win the gospel of Jesus Christ a hearing in ways seldom achieved by sheer "proclamation."

At the Outset of the Third Millennium, the Spiritual Condition of Humankind Seems One of . . . Despair

Jesus counseled his disciples to "discern the signs of the times." By this he meant not only that they should be keen observers of the events, trends, and goals of their contemporaries but also that they should seek to intuit, beneath externalities, the most deeply motivating "spirit of the age," its *zeitgeist*. The authenticity of any church's mission will depend in large measure upon the sensitivity of its reading of the spiritual climate prevailing in its worldly situation.

One of the most significant developments in recent theology has been the recognition of the *contextual* nature of all Christian thought. We have spent time in this seminar deliberately listening to, and trying to understand, one another's sociohistorical contexts. Precisely out of this exercise in honoring difference, there has emerged the consensus that the prevailing mood of humankind, *globally* considered, must be named "despair."

Despair means literally the negation, diminution, or dearth of hope (*spes*). In the absence of a public expectancy strong enough to generate viable policies of meaning and direction, human beings and communities are abandoned to the mercies of leaderless systems, unquestioned "necessities," and false promises. The modern vision, the rhetoric of which still informs much of the public life of the world's possessing peoples, has failed visibly. Although its failure is cushioned by the present (and likely temporary) economic and technological successes of the so-called developed world, the condition of the dispossessed peoples of the planet is worsened by the incapacity of the possessing peoples for either self-knowledge or planetary responsibility. There is a clear connection between the *hidden* despair of those who "have" and the *open* despair of those who do not. By far the more problematic form of despair, on account of both its repressive character and the questionable foundations of its assumed optimism, is the covert despair of the affluent. The greatest test of the Christian message in our time is whether it is able to engage and transform *that* despair.

Christian Hope Is "Hope against Hope"

If we articulate the calling of the Christian movement today in the language of hope, it is because we cannot ignore the reality of worldly despair and the melancholy future that it evokes. Only a new and lively hope—one that does not have to ignore the data of despair—can deliver humankind from the oblivion that is being courted by its unthinking pursuit of "progress" through technological mastery. The Earth will not bear such plunder, nor will the poor of the Earth for long submit to the "redundancy" to which the plundering few reduce them! Christian hope is hope "against" all the false hopes of those who do not reckon with the reality of a limited biosphere and a shared existence.

As we draw upon the biblical language of hope, we are conscious of the tendency of those most committed to the modern experiment to confuse hope with optimism. In both its Marxist and its capitalist expressions, modernity assumed that the redemptive factor was inherent in the historical process as such—that progress for all was inevitable. But biblical faith does not regard divine Providence as a synonym for historical progress. The redemptive dimension, for this faith, is inherent in neither history nor nature; it is introduced into time from beyond the potentiality of time for healing and wholeness (*shalom*). *God*, graciously and apart from all deserving, offers us a future that our own past does not warrant. God's future breaks, continuously, the dread patterns of cause and effect in which, both personally and corporately, we languish. The hope that is God's gift to faith is therefore precisely *hope*—not sight, not inevitability, not finality. It must be grasped and implemented by the community of faith and by all who, from whatever sources of longing, imagination, and common grace, glimpse possibilities for what is *new*. It must become hope *in action*.

Again, we are conscious of the propensity of "religion," Christianity not excepted, to relegate the object of hope to a realm beyond this life. Without denying the transcendent dimension of Christian hope, we nevertheless insist upon the primacy of its world orientation. "God so loved *the world*. . . ." In Jesus Christ, God intends the "mending" of creation, not its surpassing. In the words of Dietrich Bonhoeffer, "This world must not be prematurely abandoned." The hope that the divine Spirit breathes into our often skeptical and reluctant spirits translates itself ever anew into ethically concrete behavior whose object is to implement God's love for the world and all its creatures. Christians do not expect to perfect the world, but they do expect and hope to change it. Our mission as Christ's disciple community, wherever we are located, is nothing more or less than to participate actively in this divine labor of faithful love. That is to say . . .

Christian Mission Is Not First
Christian Mission but God's Mission (*Missio Dei*)

The triune God, Creator, Redeemer, Sanctifier, is "at work in the world to make and to keep human life human" (Paul Lehmann). Because God's humanizing labor is shrouded in the mystery of the Trinity, no one people, race, or faith tradition may claim to represent it fully or exclusively. We believe that the Christian movement is indeed one of the vehicles of God's transforming work in the world, and we call all Christians to believe and appropriate this with all their hearts, minds, souls, and physical abundance. Yet we know, as well, that the church is an imperfect witness to God's reign, and our experience of the Holy Spirit is such that we know that we are not alone in seeking to participate in the providential labor of God.

As the church sheds some of the institutional garments with which its status as religious establishment clothed it, and as Christian communities recover something of the movement-quality (*communio viatorum*) of the New Testament *koinonia*, Christians everywhere are beginning to recognize the companionable presence of many others who, even if they do not move with us in obvious ways, are nevertheless in close proximity and seem to be journeying in the same direction. In a world in which daily life is determined by indifference to ultimate questions and in which the future is being shaped by economic and other forces that do not concern themselves with humanity's "chief end," the presence of genuine faith in many different forms constitutes a source of courage and a confirmation of hope. In our own always inadequate attempts to live as those "sent" by a just and compassionate God, we are becoming more and more grateful for the solidarity of others who, in their own ways, manifest an apostolic vocation. In particular, we cherish the increasing mutuality and support of our parental faith, Judaism, from whose faithful spokespersons we Christians still have much to learn about the world-directedness of God's mission and the prophetic calling of God's people.

Christian Hope Is Hope *in Action*

Christian faith can never be satisfied with a theology of hope that is purely attitudinal, abstract, or "doctrinal." Such hope drives toward specificity in deed and word. By definition, the consequences of this hope are inexhaustible. In order to avoid generalization, however, we want to propose the following as instances of the concrete actions to which our contemplation of Christian mission today impels us:

1. Intentional Evangelical Emphases within the Churches

The necessity for rethinking the nature of Christian mission comes at a time when the churches, on the whole, are ill prepared for such a challenge. For many, the Bible, which with the Reformers we regard as the primary textual authority of faith, is virtually an unknown book. Doctrinal traditions that evolved over two thousand years of trial and error are neglected or trivialized, when they are not completely ignored. Spirituality, which in the best traditions of the faith is understood as the struggle of the Holy Spirit to communicate with our mostly unreceptive spirits, is too often reduced to vague feelings of bourgeois contentment or private piety.

It is pointless to call Christian congregations to a new and earnest apostolicity when they themselves are only superficially interested in the substance of the faith or are confused about scripture, doctrine, and the history and present reality of the ecumenical church. For the most part, at least in the former strongholds of Christendom, it is very hard to distinguish Christians from the social strata to which they belong.

Wherever it is located, the Christian movement will be able to *confess* hope in action only where it has been enabled through sound teaching and preaching to *profess* Christian faith. The church is in a position to *engage* its context only where it does not simply *reflect* its context. Perhaps for the foreseeable future, therefore, the rule, especially in the once-mainline churches of former Christendom, ought to be: In the church tell the story, in the world live the story.

2. Developing Prophetic Consciousness

As Western churches find themselves pushed toward the margins of their societies, there is a new opportunity for the development of an autonomous critical awareness. In the post-Christendom situation, when Christians are liberated *from* the obligation of upholding and legitimating all the "values" of their host cultures, they are simultaneously liberated *for* a greater and more sensitive awareness of the world at large, particularly those whose destiny is adversely affected by the exclusionary side of global economics.

The affluent nations have embraced a lifestyle that places unreasonable and dangerous demands upon the biosphere, entails the endless and often pointless technologization of society, and is driven by a market ideology that excludes and oppresses the vast majority of the planet's human and extra-human inhabitants. In particular, the events of history have conspired to fashion of the United States of America the only remaining "superpower," an imperium from which profit-driven systems emanate, including a technologically sophisticated popular culture that supplants indigenous cultures and ancient traditions. The United States itself, including not only its cultural heritage but also its democratic ideals, is threatened by the power of this new imperialism.

We therefore urge American, Canadian, European, and other Christians among the possessing peoples to develop greater vigilance for the injustice resultant upon the uncurbed and rampant career of global technopoly. Indifference and apathy are tempting wherever people seem to benefit from such a system, but in the long run no one will benefit! There are traditions of justice, peace, self-criticism, simplicity, and compassion in the West—perhaps *especially* in the United States—upon which Christians may and must draw in their attempts to turn the policies of their countries toward a greater responsibility for the whole earth and all of its inhabitants. Whatever our nation, our vocation as Christians entails the stewardly care of all creation, and in this we gladly make common cause with all persons and communities of faith and good will who seek the well-being of God's beloved world.

3. Broadening Theological Education

Conscious of the gaps and omissions in our own preparation for ministry, we urge theological educators to broaden and deepen the exposure of candidates for ministry to the worldwide character of the Christian movement today and to the faiths of other people. Historically, Christianity is inextricably bound up with the history and culture of Europe and its colonies; for that reason, no genuine introduction to the Christian faith either can or should seek to avoid the European connection. At the same time, present-day Christianity exists, and sometimes flourishes, in places far removed from European history and culture. All who experience something of the wider, truly ecumenical church (as we have done in this seminar!) know that their faith can be only enriched by such exposure. A theological education centered exclusively or chiefly in Eurocentric thought is no adequate preparation for ministry and mission in the twenty-first century.

Similarly, it does not threaten the uniqueness of the Christian witness to enter into dialogue with Muslim, Buddhist, Hindu, and other believers, including those who attempt today to keep alive the religions of indigenous peoples the world over. To the contrary, in our concourse with these others we can come to know not only *their* faiths but also *our own*, in ways unknown to persons who remain with the confines of their own religious traditions. We may also find, in such dialogue, points of commonality in both theology and ethics, and so expand our conception of the *missio Dei*.

The record of informed conversation and interaction between Christians and persons of other faiths (even Judaism!) is shockingly meager. It is unlikely that this will be altered in the near future unless, already in seminaries, future "teaching elders" are introduced to religious plurality in a serious and sustained manner.

4. Toward a Truly Ecumenical Stewardship of Christian Resources

The mission of the church does not rest with one segment or province of the church but belongs to the whole Body of Christ, with each part contributing according to its ability and receiving according to its need. Given the present and future shift of majority forms of the Christian faith to the Southern Hemisphere, and given the asymmetrical nature of the financial and material resources of the ecumenical church, it is imperative that more of these resources should be directed toward the churches and educational institutions of the south. The course of Christianity within the present century and beyond will be greatly influenced by the work and witness of Christians in Africa, Asia, and Latin America. Particularly with respect to theological education, resources both financial and educational are badly needed in these contexts. It will go a long way toward ensuring a responsible Christian mission if this challenge is taken up by the more affluent churches of the Northern Hemisphere, which could consider such action a genuine expression of their hope. With exceptions, it would appear that churches of the south do not need more "missionaries" from the north; rather, they need the wherewithal to educate their own missionaries and to support the missions they have themselves put in place.

Christians in the south as well as Christians in the north are challenged to resist the "Christianizing" tendencies of triumphalistic forms of the faith. As the number of Christians in the south continues to grow at a remarkable rate, churches are facing the formidable task of living up to mission as hope *in action*. This means confessing hope in contexts of depressing suffering, hardening poverty, the growing scourge of AIDS, the legacy of "Christian" Western subjugation, and simmering ethnoreligious conflicts. Here the enactment of Christian hope entails participation in the harsh realities of daily existence, where choices are being made between life and death. As the number of Christians in the Southern Hemisphere increases, there is a corresponding need to ensure that faith in Jesus Christ issues in a responsible, this-worldly mission.

5. The Abiding Question

The one-page statement that was given to all participants in this seminar prior to their arrival in Decatur ends in the following, sobering way: "It is an open question whether the church can be, or become, unfettered to face the present summons of the gospel, given its careless, long-standing enmeshment in the fearfulness and anxiety of the world." This question remains. We have not answered it. We cannot answer it. It will be answered, day by day, year by year, decade by decade, in one way or another—whether in the positive or in the negative. All that we can do, beyond articulating our own hope, is to suggest that no *desirable* answer will be given to this question unless those who are now and in the future being prepared for ministry are helped already in their seminary training to distinguish between the historical accidents of our Christendom past and the essence of the faith that is testified to by the Holy Spirit, the only trustworthy interpreter of both scripture and tradition. The "unfettering" of the church begins at that point where human beings who feel themselves beckoned to follow the Christ realize in their hearts that the times of culture-Christianity—Christianity based on inheritance and convention—are over, that from now on all who follow this Way must be prepared to give a reason for the hope that is in them.

This is a far cry from the time-honored conventions of a professional clergy. It is nothing less than a call to radical discipleship—quite possibly to suffering. That such a thing might be considered unusual only reminds us how far we have come from Christian beginnings. In those beginnings, participation in the *mission* of Christ meant participation in Christ's *passion*. As it was in the beginning, is now, and ever shall be! The only enduring "mark of the true church" is the presence in it of the holy cross (Luther).

* * *

For eight weeks, we have met together in worship, prayer, and expectation of the Word and Spirit of God. Now our study draws to an end, and we are pleased to be able to submit to you this summary of our common findings. We do so with high respect for the enterprise in theological education being conducted at Columbia Theological Seminary, an enterprise that we have glimpsed through our contacts with many of you throughout the course of these weeks. Please be assured of our sincere and lasting gratitude for the Christian hospitality, kindness, courtesy, and friendship that we have been shown during the entire period of our sojourn in your midst. May God continue to bless your community of learning and prayer.

Part Two

Chances for Hope
Made Context-Specific

Chapter Three

Atlanta as Church Context

Joanna Adams

In literature, the concept of setting (the word *setting* being a synonym for what is today usually referred to as "context") includes the dual aspects of time and place. These seem to be helpful categories for thinking about some of the distinctive, even peculiar, aspects of the situation in which I and the congregation I serve seek to live out our calling of discipleship.

Our Time

Our time is one in which people appear to be searching for meaning with renewed urgency. Despite many late-twentieth-century predictions to the contrary, they are pursuing that search by means of religious faith and practices more vigorously than ever. Because there are more choices of ways for people to address their spiritual hungers, there is a tendency on the part of many to cobble together a variety of beliefs and rituals. I am reminded of the church member who came to visit me not long after I had been called to serve her congregation as pastor. She wanted to find out what my understanding of reincarnation was and whether I thought it had a place in the belief system of the Christian faith. When I responded that Christianity knew nothing of reincarnation but had resurrection as its central claim, she hastily left my office and thereafter withdrew completely from the life of the church.

Although six of ten Americans claim to attend church each week, there is an increasing lack of knowledge about the Bible and the central tenets of Christianity.

The idea that the purpose of human life is to glorify God is a decidedly alien notion in a culture that is centered on the self. Deep commitment to serving the purposes of God in the broader realms of society has been supplanted by a strong emphasis on personal spiritual fulfillment.

There is a dramatic decline of interest in denominationalism on the part of many who seek the fellowship of the church; there is also a glaring lack of knowledge as to the basic history and beliefs of the tradition on the part of many who are already active participants.

Technology is dramatically changing how much and with whom a faith community is able to communicate. The website of the church I serve in Atlanta averages thousands of "hits" per month, from people all around the country, as well as from its membership. One can now log on to the website and choose either to read or to listen to the Sunday sermon.

There is unprecedented growth among evangelical and Pentecostal churches in America, while the mainline Christian churches continue a general numerical decline. Nine of ten missionaries sent to other parts of the world from North America are evangelical or Pentecostal.

A paradox exists at this juncture in the American religious experience. On the one hand, there appears to be a good bit of anti-intellectualism, emotionalism, and superficiality associated with the more popular forms of American Christianity today. At the same time, Christian theologians and ethicists are making indispensable contributions to the conversation in genetic science and in the public debates about individual morality and the search for the common good. Surely, Christian churches have a crucial responsibility to provide forums for moral discourse on the great issues that face society at the beginning of a new millennium.

Our Place

Atlanta, which began as a rough-and-ready railroad town and was originally named Terminus, is now a megacity without equal in the southeastern United States. It is said that the Atlanta metropolitan area has experienced the most dramatic expansion of real estate development in the shortest span of time of any metropolis in history. The consequences of this growth have been dramatic. The economy is booming. Unemployment is at its lowest level in thirty years. Opportunity and prosperity abound for many. But the consequences are not all positive. The "rising tide lifts all boats" approach to economic development has not worked for many. Homelessness, inadequate housing, low wages, and hunger are everyday realities for them. The income gap between the rich and the poor continues to widen. Streets, boulevards, and interstate highways are clogged with traffic. Air and water pollution are at crisis levels.

Because our city's population has become strikingly diverse in terms of ethnic identity and religious identity, no longer can homogeneity of perspective or background be assumed. As in many other regions of the United States, however, the role of religion is becoming increasingly confined to the private spheres of life and is commonly considered to be irrelevant to the issues that affect public life. The secular values of individualism, consumerism, and success are now the values that prevail.

Race continues to be the predominant factor in determining many of the patterns of community life and practice.

Economic disparities loom equally as large. Two important questions arise from this final consideration:

- How can the affluent and the relatively affluent receive the gift of God's future if their hands are full of the fruits of their own success and their minds are full of their own plans?
- How can those who have been left out of the prosperity—or who are struggling not to be—receive the gift of God's future if despair has depleted their capacity for hope?

Chapter Four

South Africa
and the Confession of Belhar

A Contemporary Confessing
Journey toward Mission

H. Russel Botman

The Barmen Declaration (1934) and the Confession of Belhar (1986) have played formative roles in the making and unmaking of ecclesial and political life in Germany and South Africa. Their continuing relevance as contemporary confessions is evident in the many studies done about them internationally and in the fact that churches in other countries have decided to include them in their confessional heritage.

Belhar and Barmen have become "symbols of liberation" (John De Gruchy) in two different contexts where Christians had to respond to a *status confessionis*. Despite their symbolic congruence, the Declaration of Barmen and the Confession of Belhar differ in many ways. Barmen presents itself as a theological declaration true to the Word of God, whereas Belhar considers itself a confession. The Barmen Declaration is a text with six theses on "evangelical truths" central to the situation of its time in the Nazi regime, and Belhar consists of five clauses embedded in its confessional struggle against apartheid.[1]

This characteristic Christology of Belhar consequentially focuses strongly on discipleship. This means that its five confessional clauses must be read as practices the church is called to doing in its discipleship (*imitatio Christi*). Just as Barmen does, it first confesses faith in the triune God. However, it goes further in identifying the practices of such a God: "who collects, defends and cares for his Church by his Word and Spirit." Second, Belhar speaks about the unity of the church in Jesus Christ, which means that believers should "experience, practice and pursue community with one another" in freedom and not under constraint. Third, it states what the people believe regarding reconciliation and connects it to the responsibility of the church to act in reconciliation. The fourth clause centralizes the focus of justice expressed as discipleship. The fifth section refers to costly practices of absolute obedience to God.

The question faced in a postapartheid context is, How are we now called to confess and what are we called to confess in mission?

In 1996, I chaired a historic consultation of African scholars on the issue of "how our faith is being challenged by economic globalization" in Kitwe, Zambia, where a new, groundbreaking theological awareness arose. This consultation proposed that Africa is faced with a *status confessionis* in the light of the exclusionary nature of economic globalization. This matter was referred to the executive of the World Alliance of Reformed Churches (WARC) for ecumenical evaluation and action.

Urged by the Southern African Alliance of Reformed Churches (SAARC), of which I was the moderator at the time, the executive of WARC allowed time for a special forum of churches from the south, which was to be sponsored by SAARC on the evening of Wednesday, August 13, 1997. On that evening, I outlined three reasons why the WARC is not yet ready to declare a *status confessionis* on global economic injustice. The alliance (a) does not have a shared plausible theological category to judge the current global economic reality; (b) although it has so many member churches from the south in its consciousness, the alliance does not come from an illuminating contextual position to understand the *kairos,* as a result of the overarching power of the north; and (c) I questioned whether it had the combined missional or political will to act on this matter in the nature of a confessing community. From the perspective of the south, the question is no longer whether we are in a *status confessionis* of a global economic nature. However, based on the criteria required for the declaration of such a state of confession, we must conclude that it is not yet possible in worldwide Christianity. The WARC, therefore, declared a process of learning, education, confession, and action at this time in history.

Based on the recommendation of Section II, the WARC, at its meeting in Debrecen, Hungary, 1997, subsequently declared a *processus confessionis* with regard to economic justice in the context of globalization.

> In the past we have called for *status confessionis* in cases of blatant racial and cultural discrimination and genocide. WE NOW

CALL FOR A COMMITTED PROCESS OF PROGRES-
SIVE RECOGNITION, EDUCATION AND CONFES-
SION (*PROCESSUS CONFESSIONIS*) WITHIN ALL WARC
MEMBER CHURCHES AT ALL LEVELS REGARDING
ECONOMIC INJUSTICE AND ECOLOGICAL DESTRUC-
TION. (Proceedings of the Twenty-third General Council of the
WARC, held in Debrecen, Hungary, August 8–20, 1997, p. 198;
their capital letters)

The alliance has invited member churches and Christians everywhere to embark on a journey in which we continue to study the
global phenomenon and its impact on people and nature to come to
a better understanding of the theological center of the global challenge, which could lead to faithful action for global transformation.

The great learning and collaborative experience that I could share
with others in the Campbell Seminar brought me back to the theological importance of the term *confess* for the mission of the church.
This is what makes the mission of the church unique, that it is a conscious form of confession. The energy of South African Christianity
in the antiapartheid struggle arose from its understanding that the
church's mission is a confession. If we have to ask what we should confess in the twenty-first century, Africa has identified the reality of
global economic injustice as a center for such mission. Confessing
hope in action would mean translating this ethical issue into its confessional meaning in order for us to act on it.

The Confession of Belhar is one resource that we might use in
developing such a mission.

Chapter Five

The Canadian Context

Douglas John Hall

Canada is a very big place! As a country, it covers a territory second in size only to Russia. As a modern nation, it dates to the Confederation of 1867, but its beginnings as a European colony are in the sixteenth century. Martin Luther was at the height of his career when the first European-style musical concert was given in the village that became my city, Montreal. New France predates New England by a hundred years.

The character of the country is bound up with its being the product of two founding peoples (French and English) building on the base of an indigenous people, whose presence is still very much felt. The "two solitudes," as one of our great writers termed English and French cultures, have never dwelt together amiably, and tensions have been strong since the development in the 1960s of the separatist movement in Quebec. Yet the two cultures have profoundly influenced one another, and most Canadians would feel, I think, that something of the essence of Canada was missing, were Quebec actually to go its own way.

The most decisive factor in recent Canadian experience has been the ubiquitous and unrelenting influence of the United States, our powerful southern neighbor, with whom our destiny has been bound up from the outset but that today, in consequence of "global" economics (two-thirds of it American) and modern communications, constitutes a very serious threat to our future as a nation. On the one hand, this means the sheer economic clout of an imperial power: Canada owns a smaller proportion of its productive capacity than any other industrialized nation. On the other hand, the threat is broadly cultural: 88 percent of the TV that Canadians watch comes directly from the United States, to mention only one of the ways in which American pop culture is transmitted across the border.

The result is a steady but measurable erosion of Canadian identity and autonomy. A recent national weekly edition of the *Washington Post* (Oct. 2, 2000) asks in its lead article, "How Much Longer for Canada?" Some would like to attribute the tenuousness of our country to French-English relations, but that is much too simple. The real problem, as the late Pierre Trudeau once famously stated it, is that Canada is a mouse in bed with an elephant—the United States.

Traditionally, however, Canada never wanted to become "America North." There are some important differences that some of us may die trying to preserve! I will name four of these. First, Canada has manifested an unusual hospitality to diversity. Of course, we are not free of prejudice; other races have not always had an easy time of it, nor have the indigenous "Indian" peoples. Compared with many other contexts, however, including the United States, Canada has a rather remarkable record of acceptance and inclusion. This is due in part, certainly, to the fact of there being not one but *two* founding cultures and languages. Canada never aspired to the U.S. melting pot philosophy; we think of ourselves, rather, as a "vertical mosaic" or a "patchwork quilt." It is possible for national groupings to retain a good deal of their own cultures. Hospitality to difference also pertains to Canada's increasingly "liberal" laws respecting gay and lesbian persons, same-sex marriages or unions, employment policies, employee benefits, and the like.

Second, Canadian history and social policy bear witness to a strong social conciousness. In this immense land, which is not always hospitable to human enterprise, people had to cooperate from the outset. From the cooperative movements, especially in western Canada, and from our ties to British socialism, there emerged a strong socialist party (the New Democratic party) that has governed several of our provinces and has forced the more dominant political parties to adopt social legislation that respects the disadvantaged, including universal medical care. Canadians are apt to be astonished when they experience U.S. politics at close hand (as at the present time of presidential election), for they hear very little by way of real difference between the two main parties. On the question of the death penalty, for example, both candidates in the present race for the White House are quick to endorse it. In Canada, the death penalty was done away with decades ago. By the way, it will surprise most Americans to learn that our socialist party was founded chiefly by Methodist and Baptist clergy and that it attracts the largest number of votes among clergy of all the mainline churches.

Third, like most northern peoples, Canadians traditionally have shown a certain typical skepticism. We are suspicious of ideology, including religious ideology and including also the American dream, of which we could simulate only a very pale version. Canadians do not "believe" easily. When you are living on a rock (the Canadian Shield!) and it's so very cold, you don't trust easy answers. I have always found this religiously very significant. Biblical faith is not "easy" either; it is not credulity. In consequence, we are by comparison with our southern neighbor a very "secular" society. Nearly 90 percent of Canadians tell the census taker that they are "Christian," but only about 20 percent go to church. "The end of Christendom" is visible among us, as in Europe. One can lament the crasser results of this, but many of us find it both more realistic and more evocative theologically that our fellow citizens no longer go in for culture-Christianity.

Fourth, there is an international awareness in Canada that I find shockingly absent in the United States. Not only does the Canadian government strongly support the United Nations but also we initiated (under Lester B. Pearson) the modern concept of conflict management through the deployment of peacekeeping forces. Ties with both "motherlands" are strong, though not always cordial, and throughout the Cold War Canada sustained working relations with many second world (Warsaw Pact) countries, including Cuba, from which our country never severed its relations. Commonwealth, Francophone and other ties have kept us in touch with many parts of the planet neglected by the superpowers, and because of our location "on the edge of empire"—an empire with which we have continued to maintain very friendly relations—Canada is able to act in an intermediary way, often, that may prevent misunderstandings and heal divisions. The CBC and (to a lesser extent) private media keep Canadians informed about the world in a manner that is simply not duplicated in the United States. It is not that Canadians are more virtuous than Americans; it's only that we are infinitely less powerful—and so less tempted by the pretensions and the myopia of power.

These things having been noted, however, it is necessary to go on and admit: every one of these four "differences"—and others that could be mentioned—is disappearing *rapidly*. In the past decade, we have even seen the emergence of a strong political party, now the party of opposition in Parliament, that mirrors almost exactly American politics of the right, with its fiscal conservativism, individualism, suspicion of social welfare, *and* its fundamentalist Christian backing.

The problem for Canada is not the United States as such and immediately; it is the subtle changes in national character and spirit, including historical and cultural amnesia, that are wrought by the allure of American power and prosperity. In short, the *will to be*—to be a country, to be different from the United States, to be true to our own traditions and established customs—this is what is being eroded. As one Canadian author put it in the title of a book, *Canada: Cancelled for Lack of Interest*. Particularly among the "English" segment of the country (which includes many recent immigrants as well as old-stock British descendants), a kind of forgetfulness has set in since the end of World War II. If Quebec separatism flourishes, as it still does, it is in large measure because it finds in English-speaking Canada so little that is genuinely Canadian. Quebec's motto is "*Je me souviens!*" (I remember). Anglo-Canada, increasingly, forgets.

As a Christian, I am an internationalist: "God so loved *the world*. . . ." But I am also a Canadian nationalist *because I am a Christian internationalist*. I have witnessed, during my 72 years, many ways in which a Canada sufficiently distinguishable from "America" can be of service to the world at large. We are not one of the great powers, but perhaps we have a destiny that is more important, ultimately, than that of being a great power: namely, that of being a serving people, a stewardly people. Our very positioning in the contemporary world, both geographically and politically, gives us just such an opportunity for service.

Perhaps one cannot ask a nation to divest itself of its own power urges sufficiently to serve. But Canadian pretension to power, given our actual status as "mouse alongside elephant," is in any case always rather ludicrous. At least the Christians among us, together with others of (international) good will, ought to do everything in our power to help our country become what it—potentially—is.

Chapter Six

Prophecy and Servanthood in the South

James S. Lowry

The context in which I have developed my theological thought and practice has been in places and institutions of the Presbyterian Church[2] in the southeastern region of the United States. I grew up, almost literally, in the Great Falls Presbyterian Church in the small community of Great Falls, South Carolina; as a teen, I participated in leadership roles at the presbytery, synod, and general assembly levels of my, then, southern denomination; I earned my undergraduate degree at Presbyterian College in Clinton, South Carolina; I received my theological education at Columbia Theological Seminary in Decatur, Georgia, the host institution of this seminar; and I have served as pastor of Presbyterian congregations in Alabama, Florida, South Carolina, Tennessee, and North Carolina.

During my childhood and youth, I sat at the feet of the Rev. Ellis L. Oakes, who was our pastor and friend. He was an excellent scholar and modeled for me the importance of serious scholarship to preaching. My theological education, both at Presbyterian College and Columbia Seminary, was heavily influenced by neo-orthodoxy and critical methods of Bible study. In recent years, however, while remaining profoundly thankful for that theological grounding, I have moved more and more in the direction of using biblical and extrabiblical narrative not only to inform and express my work as a practicing pastor and preacher but also to form that work.

Issues surrounding race and racial injustice have greatly influenced my ministry over the last thirty-four years. Moreover, changes in mission surrounding those same issues over that period represent clear and important shifts in contextual paradigm that go far beyond those concerns. For example, in the early years, following my ordination in

1966, it was important for me and the congregations I served to have a strong prophetic voice. Later, as laws and customs in the United States gradually changed, there came the necessity for me and the congregations I served to shift from prophet to servant, wherein pastor and congregation reached out in service to the poor in the community, a disproportionate number of whom were and are African Americans. In more recent years, there has been yet another shift. Now, the emphasis is on mutuality, wherein there is a concern not so much about service to as service with African Americans. That shift, seen in bold relief in one set of issues, applies to virtually every aspect of Christian mission as I have experienced it.

Although race issues may represent paradigm shifts in my context for mission, the demands of preaching and worship leadership represent that which is constant in my context for mission. Most of what I have learned in the last three and a half decades has been through the eyes of one who returns weekly to holy scripture in an effort to discover there the truth of God to be interpreted and told in the community of God's people as God's people gather to worship. I sometimes find that work exhausting. I have never found it boring. To the contrary, I have always taken the task as one who is filled with wonder and amazement at it all.

I am deeply grateful to Columbia Seminary for seeing it as important that preaching pastors be given respected places and honored voices at the table of scholars gathered for these important conversations.

Chapter Seven

An Asian Context

Damayanthi M. A. Niles

Asian Christians have two realities that we hold in common. We, with the notable exception of the Philippines, are all minorities in our countries. Because of this reality, it is becoming increasingly difficult for us as Christians to see ourselves apart from the people of other religions. Therefore, the contours of relationships between us and people of other faiths have to be and are being redrawn.

The second reality we hold in common as Asians is that we are still caught up in defining who we are apart from and in relation to the colonial powers that ruled us and subjugated us to their worldview. Politically, morally, aesthetically, socially, and historically, we struggle to define ourselves rather than to react and respond to Western ideas of how the world should be visualized, constructed, and run. Even in the language of postcolonialism, while trying to deconstruct colonial and neocolonial ways of thinking, we continue to build a definition of ourselves negatively, rather than making a positive claim about who we are.

Because of these two realities there are two interacting issues that have been, and must continue to be, addressed by Asian theology: Christ-centered relationships to other faiths and Asian Christian cultural identity. We are Christians; therefore, the figure of Jesus Christ shapes our thinking and the way we respond to and live in the world. Christ-centered language is a simple acknowledgment of that fact. We are also Asian, and the cultures from which we come also shape who we understand ourselves to be, not only as people but also as Christian people.

Because the only way we can speculate about where we are going in the future is to look at where we have been in the past, I want to look at how these issues have been used to respond to the realities of religious plurality and colonial identity in the Asian theological movement.

The first stage in the Asian theological movement was toward the particular. It was based on the belief that to understand what ecumenical life is, you must start with particular situations, rather than universal concepts. It featured focusing on people of a particular culture, rather than theological anthropology in a more universal abstract form. Rather than construct doctrines about human sinfulness and *imago Dei*, it attempted to understand God's people in their concrete reality. It was a spiritual journey to rediscover Christ in the midst of the people.

This stage of the movement also took seriously the resources found in a culture as a means of deciphering how a culture understands and articulates itself and its relationship to the Divine. There was a change in the language of theology from discourse—drawing conclusions from given doctrinal positions—to the language of confession, story, doxology, and poetry that is attempting to capture the experience of the Divine's interaction with a particular moment.

This was done in several ways. First, the movement began to widen the theological and missiological horizon. At the Edinburgh Conference of 1910, the plea of Bishop Azariah of India and Cheng Chung-Yu of China to "send us friends" was a step in claiming the right to an Asian Christian identity. It was a request to the Western churches to cease treating the churches in the East as domains for mission and instead see them as partners. It was the movement of seeing Asian Christians as the people of Christ who are involved in articulating and shaping the church and its history, rather than the objects of mission enterprise. At Tambaram in 1938, Justice P. Chenchiah moved us toward a new understanding of what it means to be God's people by protesting the use of the fear of syncretism as a means to ghettoizing *missio Dei* in *missio ecclesia* and arguing that other faiths have a place in understanding God's work in the world.

Second, the movement began to break the umbilical cord and steer away from the dependent need to justify ourselves in the Western theological and missiological arena toward a confidence to discern the divine in our own midst. This meant looking to Asian resources as a key for understanding and articulating our Christian beliefs.

Now, however, we are ready to move on to a new stage of the theological movement. We can no longer stay simply with the particular. A wider conversation needs to take place if we are to avoid two pitfalls. One is becoming focused on a psychology of victimization, in which we become so focused on our pain that it becomes the only thing that defines us and we fall into the futile argument of who has the most pain as the means of stating who is closest to God. The second pitfall is the danger of becoming ghettoized in genetically confined theological conversations, which assumes that the only theology we can understand is the one we are biologically related to.

There is a need to broaden the ecumenical horizon by asking the simple yet profound question, *Are there not other partners in our ecumenical search?* Where do we go to find other sources to help make a wider theological conversation possible? From Asia alone, there are partners from other faiths and traditions, the church that arose from the missionary work of St. Thomas and his disciples, and the context we live in, which functions as a text that must interact with the biblical text we have inherited. As we broaden the discussion further, other partners come into play in such forms as postmodern and postcolonial discourse.

We are now at a point of searching for a more satisfactory and more satisfying understanding of ecumenical life. Please note that we are not talking about defining ecumenism. We are looking for a new style of loving that cares for all the richness of our religions and cultures and brings these as contributions to a larger, richer dialogue of life.

Chapter Eight

The Cuban Church in Socialism

Ofelia Ortega

The First Period: "Zeal" (1959–1960)

It is a well-known fact that at the beginning of the revolutionary process in Cuba (January 1, 1959), our churches were undergoing a time of despair. We did not know what to do. We were not actually prepared to face the challenge of the structural changes in our society. Enrique Dussel in his *History of the Church in Latin America (1492–1992)*[3] establishes a clear division into periods of the events that characterize each of the stages of the relationship between the church and the revolution in Cuba. On January 29, 1959, the Cuba Episcopate issued a circular letter of critical character, "In the face of the firing-squad executions." From February 13 to 18, it advocated private school education. On May 17, it warned against socialism in the laws of the Agrarian Reform. Finally, it organized the National Catholic Congress that closed on November 29 before the revered image of the Virgin Mary of the Caridad del Cobre (Charity of Copper). Monseñor Enrique Pérez Serante, who in 1956 defended Fidel Castro and saved his life after the attack on Moncada Garrison, presided at the meeting. Commander-in-Chief Fidel Castro himself was also present. Shouts were heard: "*Cristo sí, otro no*" (Yes to Christ, No to other) and "*Cuba sí, Rusia no*" (Yes to Cuba, No to Russia). Consejo Episcopal Latin Americano (CELAM) itself, in its Fourth Assembly in Fomeque, Colombia, on November 19, condemned "the delusions of Communism" and the "incompatibility of Communism and Christianity."

On August 7, 1960, a collective circular letter of the Cuban Episcopate declared that "the absolute majority of the Cuban people, who are Catholics, only through delusion could be led to a communist regime." The real estate possessions of the church were affected by

45

the urban reform from September 14, as properties were confiscated and rents lowered in favor of the impoverished masses.

The Second Period: "Confrontation" (1961–1967)

It started with Castro's speech on June 2, 1960, as he declared: "Whosoever is anticommunist is then anti-revolutionary." The Christian leaders of the bourgeoisie and the petite bourgeoisie moved over en masse to the opposition. There began the immigration to Miami and the enrollment of many in conspiracy actions against the government.

The Reformed-Presbyterian Church (my church) lost two-thirds of its congregations, who left for the United States of America. Only fourteen out of forty-one pastors remained in the country. In such a situation, the witness of the church in our society was impoverished as a consequence of an ecclesiastic practice that responded to a culture of domination.

On June 6, 1961, the schools were nationalized, the currency was annulled, and the cemeteries were confiscated. The procession of the Virgin Mary of the Charity of Copper (Virgen de la Caridad del Cobre) was repressed on September 8, and the chain of events ended with the expulsion of 133 priests on September 12. Among these banished priests was Monseñor Francisco Oves Martínez, who was later to become Archbishop of Havana. Of 745 priests in 1960, only 230 remained in 1969; of 2,225 nuns in 1960, only about 200 remained in 1970.

The Third Period: "Evasion" and "Coexistence" (1968–1970)

It was actually a period of silence, a time of things going to their depth. The new winds of Vatican Council II were blowing. Noteworthy at this time was the presence of Monseñor César Zacchi in Havana as apostolic delegate of the Vatican, with a history of experience in the eastern socialist countries. On December 21, 1964, was the funeral of Father Guillermo García, who was buried with honors corresponding to a commander dead in battle. Father Sardiñas had fought as a member of Fidel Castro's rebel army and earned the rank of a commander. In 1959, he came back to work as a parish priest in Cristo Rey (Christ the King) Church in Havana. In 1966, San Carlos and San Ambrosio Catholic Seminary opened again. The Acción Católica

(Catholic Action) group was dissolved, and Formation, Liturgy, Apostolic, and Catechism (FLAC) was reorganized. There began preparation so that Cuba might be present in Medellín (1968), although the impact of the conference was quite limited as far as Cuba was concerned.

Sergio Arce, a Presbyterian pastor, published in 1963 a theological reflection on the vocation of the Cuban church, "The Mission of the Church in a Socialist Society." In this paper, Arce points out:

> We have to start by opening the doors of the church, go into the open space, and recognize and share the facts of the concrete human event that has taken place around us, that is, the historical phenomenon that has occurred and is still evolving in the contemporary history of our country and the world. We have to admit it, and we have to share in it. We have to take it just as it is in our case, that is, as a Marxist-Leninist Revolution. In the 20th century, it cannot be otherwise. This is the revolutionary principle of the present century. Just as in other centuries, revolution took place in the name, and under the guide and direction of other revolutionary principles.

The Fourth Period: Mutual Acknowledgment of the Need for a Dialogue (1970–1980)

This was started by Fidel Castro himself at the Congress of Intellectuals that took place in Havana. There, in the presence of five hundred leaders of the whole world, Castro stated: "Such are the paradoxes of history: sectors of the clergy are becoming more and more revolutionary forces, how is it then we will resign ourselves to see Marxist sectors become ecclesiastic forces."

On April 20, 1969, the episcopate issued a communiqué condemning the economic and political blockade organized by the United States against Cuba. On July 19, Monseñor Oves was consecrated as archbishop of Havana. On September 8, another communiqué circulated: "We have to address ourselves to the atheist with all respect and fraternal charity. . . . In the endeavor to develop and promote all and every human being, there is a vast field of common efforts to all persons of good will, regardless of whether they are believers or atheists." From April 23 to 30, 1971, there took place the National Congress of Education and Culture. From November 5 to December 4,

Fidel Castro visited Chile and had a "dialogue" with eighty priests who later visited Cuba in February 1972.

A Cuban delegation was present at Santiago de Chile to take part in the First Latin American Encounter of Christians for Socialism, which took place from March 23 to 27. Gonzalo Arroyo stated at this meeting: "The objective analysis of the Latin American political reality leads to the conviction that the repeated failures of the Left to attract the masses in a decided struggle against the national and international forces of capitalism, demands the multitudinous incorporation of Christians in the revolutionary process."

In the conclusions of the encounter, it is declared: "The construction of socialism is a creative process not compatible with any dogmatic narrow-mindedness and non-critical position. . . . In such circumstances, religion loses its character as opium for the people . . . and becomes one more inspiration factor in the struggle for peace, freedom and justice."

The relationship between Christianity and socialism began to be explicitly formulated in the Christian student groups, above all from 1959 onward, and by the Cuban revolution itself. In Cuba the term *encounter* is preferred to the term *dialogue*, as the latter is felt to have a rather theoretical connotation, and theoretical discussion has not been the fundamental fact in our experience.

The crisis in the relationships between church and revolution was gradually passing. However, the church kept itself still isolated from the renewal of the church of the poor—from the theology of liberation.

On March 27, 1974, Monseñor Agostino Casaroli visited Cuba. Monseñor César Zacchi was appointed nuncio, and in 1975 he was succeeded by Monseñor Mario Taglaferri.

In December 1975, the First Congress of the Communist Party took place. Although the intent of an open dialogue was manifest in this meeting, in practice a "dogmatic" position was still held: "science and religion opposed each other irreconcilably."

Article thirty-five of the Socialist Constitution reads: "The profession of all religions is free. . . . The Church is separated from the State, which should not subsidize any religious cult."

Two facts indicated the movement to a mutual aperture. On the one hand, there was the condemnation of the terrorist attack against the Cuban Airline, stated by the episcopate and the Cuban Council of Churches. The statement was published in *Granma Newspaper* on November 16, 1976. On the other hand, there was the dialogue with

Christian pastors in Jamaica, on October 29, 1977, on the side of Fidel Castro. This is why at the Eleventh World Festival of the Youth, in Havana, held in July 1978, Monseñor Oves had grounds to say: "The ideal of a society without economic or social antagonist classes is more in accordance with the evangelical demand for fraternity in Christ, but I ask myself: How can we help one another in making viable the Christians' commitment in the progressive realization of such ideal, if Christian faith is presented as something necessarily hostile? . . . We would like to substantiate this consideration based on the principles of Marxist social science itself, which does not detach theory from reality."

We cannot possibly fail to mention the influence exerted by the Confession of Faith of the Reformed-Presbyterian Church in Cuba, 1977, during this period. This document constitutes the first confession of faith of a national church in a socialist country, a part of the dialogue with Marxism.

The 1979 triumph of the Sandinista Revolution in Nicaragua began to show to Cuba a way in the relationship between church and revolution, as Christians took part multitudinously in the insurrection struggle and later in power.

From February 26 to March 3, 1979, the Evangelical Theological Seminary of Matanzas was the host of a historical meeting of seventy-seven theologians from socialist countries (from Europe, Asia, Africa, and Latin America) holding a dialogue about the viability of the theology of liberation in their respective places.

Fifth Period: Participation (1980–1991)

In June 1985, U. S. presidential candidate the Rev. Jesse Jackson visited the island. Fidel Castro visited the Methodist church and addressed the Christians on the occasion of a Martin Luther King day celebration meeting.

The Office of Religious Affairs by the Central Committee of the Communist Party of Cuba was created, and Dr. José Felipe Carneado was appointed head of this office.

September 1985 marked official dialogue with the Cuban Catholic bishops and visits of the Catholic bishops to the United States.

On November 14, 1985, there was official dialogue with the Ecumenical Council of Cuba, as well as elaboration of a more advanced document about Christian participation in the Cuban society, to be discussed in the Third Congress of the Communist Party of Cuba, toward the end of 1985. A million copies of the book *Fidel and Religion* were published.

On February 17 to 23, 1986, was the First National Encounter of the Cuban Catholic Church and a pastoral letter of the Cuban bishops. Religious work was opened in Cuba by Mother Teresa of Calcutta.

In April 1988, Cardinal O'Connor, Archbishop of New York, visited; he interceded for political prisoners.

In March 1990, Fidel Castro visited Brazil and criticized the Cuban church; in April, Fidel Castro met with the Ecumenical Council of Cuba to explain to the council his words in Brazil.

November 1990 was the Cuban *kairos*. The situation of the churches changed.

In December 1990, Christmas worship service was broadcast by radio.

In March 1991, there was a letter from the Episcopal Conference to Fidel Castro.

Sixth Period: Religious Rebirth in Cuba (1991–1999)

Since 1989, at a time when the so-called special period of the Cuban economy began to be foreseen and actually felt, and even more obviously in the subsequent decade of the 1990s, a religious revival has taken place in Cuba.

Some small churches have doubled their membership. Worship houses functioning as Christian churches have started to work throughout the country. Some of these worship houses even stem from denominations that have not been officially recognized and that in fact belong to what has come to be known as new religious movements.

A greater presence of the religious component has become apparent in popular music, literature, and the plastic arts. There is equally a high demand for religious literature.

Chapter Nine

Church in the Context
of Central Europe

Janos Pasztor

My American friends often wonder, How is it possible that the nations of that area are not able to settle their differences peacefully? Why is there so much strife, hatred, and bloodshed in that area? If a family lives in a large three-story house, it is easy to get away from angry exchanges by withdrawing into your own room and closing the door. If a family is crammed into a tiny flat of one or two small rooms, tensions and quarrels are inevitable. You do not have a quiet place to withdraw to.

Europe is a small continent. Central Europe is even smaller. In an area smaller than Texas, several nations live not just side by side but often in the same town or street. During the last year, I lectured at the Reformed Theological Seminary in the city of Komarno in Slovakia. It took me sixty-five minutes to get there from my home in Budapest, including crossing the border with passport and customs checks.

The geographical-historical facts are very significant. The Danube was called by the Romans *aqua contradictionis*, because at this river that flows right through central Europe various ideas, empires, and cultures had encounters, often peacefully, sometimes in bloody wars over the centuries. The Danube was the border of the Roman Empire, which represented the end of the civilized world over against the barbarian territories. Ever since, this area was a kind of bridge—or, as a Hungarian poet wrote, "ferry land"—communicating between west and east. The inhabitants have regarded themselves as part of the west but were forced to encounter with the east, having a mediatory role. That is the area, too, where the ethnic groups of Europe meet: the Latin nations on the southwest, the Saxons northwest, the Slavic nations both north and south of the river, and the Hungarians—who from the point of view of both language and physical traits differ from the rest—dividing them. For centuries, they lived side by side

51

peacefully. Trouble, war, and bloodshed were always connected with instigations from outside powers. Here has been the meeting line between eastern and western churches, including the churches of the Reformation. In the sixteenth century, because of the northern expansion of the Ottoman Empire, there was a direct encounter with Islam. The area has often suffered invasions from the east: Mongolians in the thirteenth century, Turks in the sixteenth and seventeenth, and Russians in the nineteenth and again in the twentieth. There were two invasions from the west by Austria[4] and Germany.

By the time the Hungarians—Christianized as a result of Byzantine mission—got here during the tenth century, they had to fit into the well-established pattern of European Christendom. Their ruler—later canonized by the pope as St. Stephen—opted for recognition as Christian king by the pope, avoiding thereby feudal submission to the emperors of the west and east. Fifty-five years later, the Great Schism split the church. Hungary was part of the Latin church, with a significant mediating role with the east.[5]

In the course of the nineteenth century, after much trial and tribulation, one of the most viable countries of the world, the Austro-Hungarian Empire, came into existence. It was professedly multilingual, with dynamic industrial, commercial, and cultural development, keeping the balance of power in the center of Europe. What is being worked out in the European Union in our day—including a stable common currency[6]—was already a given there.

Unfortunately, the 1920 peace dictates of Paris after World War I—resulting from the policies of some of the victorious powers, who also used the nationalist movements of the time—destroyed the empire and set up five so-called national states that were actually all multinational, but the "minorities'" rights were threatened in most cases. Apart from the inner structural tensions of these relatively small countries, their existence proved to be a power vacuum that invited the invasions of Hitler and later of the Soviet Union. These treaties sowed the seeds of World War II. Hungary suffered most, as two-thirds of its territory was taken away.[7] Because of the unsettled character of the whole situation, the others also suffered.[8]

The decision of the victorious powers to deliver central Europe to the power of the Soviet Union brought about immense suffering, as well as the destruction of democratic institutions, industry, and commerce. The cultural life of these lands, along with the atmosphere of civil society, also suffered a lot, nearly to extinction. However, these countries proved to be meat too heavy for the Soviet belly to digest. Its attempt accelerated the collapse of that regime (Berlin, 1953; Budapest, 1956; Prague, 1968; Warsaw and Gdansk, 1980).

After the collapse of the regime, these lands so plundered were not given the financial help necessary to their recovery. The victorious powers helped the adversary (Germany) in 1945 to rebuild industry and society. The same help was not given to the victims of World War II. This fact contributed to the difficulties and sufferings they endured. The standard of life in these lands is far worse than in the party-state times. The events in Romania, Albania, and Yugoslavia could have been different, too. However, the recovery has shown promising signs.

Central Europe has been part of the mainstream of European thinking and culture. These lands also contributed to the Renaissance, the Reformation, the Enlightenment, and the technological developments of the last two centuries.

That was also true of theological and church life. Central Europeans were organic parts of the dynamics of the philosophical and theological development of the whole continent.[9] In the critical years of communism, churches were able to keep in touch with the world church. After a long time, they were the first churches to live in a non-Constantinian situation without the possibility for triumphalism. In their quest for authentic theological guidance, the *ebed-pais* theology of the second and third centuries was recovered with the help of ecumenical connections. This theology was very much misused by certain individuals. However, it does serve as a biblical pattern for all churches in the post-Constantinian situation.[10]

Today, many doors have been opened for the church to witness to Christ. To carry out this mission, the church must not yield to the existing temptation of building its life and mission on the good will of the government on the Constantinian pattern or to the temptations of extreme nationalism. Today, effective mission must be carried on in the unity of word and deed by the whole people of God.

Chapter Ten

The Totalizing Context of Production and Consumption

Walter Brueggemann

I propose to understand current U.S. culture as a "totalism of productivity." By *totalism* I mean an all-comprehensive ideological system that excludes discounts and nullifies all who do not submit to that dominant ideology. By *productivity* I mean that the dominant ideological system in the United States values only those who participate in the production and consumption achievements of commodity consumerism, which is governed by the triad of money, power, and sex. The liturgies that sustain that ideology are those of sports and the entire entertainment industry, which specializes in power, success, wealth, and comfort in limitless proportion. The medium for that liturgy is, of course, television and increasingly the Internet, which mediates a world of speed, power, and growth that is completely disconnected from the lived reality of bodily persons in bodily communities.

This "virtual reality"—a totally unreal reality—constitutes a fantasy world that cuts people off from the realities of bodily existence or of the body politic. That ideology is committed to the notion of limitless entertainment without costs, especially without social costs, limitless entertainment that seeks to negate elemental communities and to nullify the political processes of hard-contested issues. It goes without saying that this ideology aims to screen out and so negate the existence of those who are nonproductive.

This ideology is at least indifferent if not hostile to every social structure and institution that is indispensable for a functioning human community:

- Commodity appetites are unlimited and make environmental concerns cranky and old-fashioned.
- Fast food and dual incomes make family nurture exceedingly difficult.

- The corporate takeover of universities plus the privatization of lower schools jeopardize education.
- The denial of death and the endless appreciation of "beauty" make the crisis of health care impossible.
- The endless supply of money makes the political process suspect and dysfunctional.

The comprehensive scope of the ideological system is so dazzling that it is difficult to conceptualize or imagine life outside this network of values.

Missional possibility in such a context is exceedingly problematic. It might include:

- The relishing of *nonproductivity* and the *nonproductive*
- The formation and nurture of *face-to-face community*
- The practice of *limit* in every aspect of life

The pastoral-liturgical task may be to help people disengage from the seductive power of that system and the decommoditization of our lives in order to be members of an alternative system. I have come to think that the recovery of Sabbath is the first sign of disengagement and alternative.

Part Three

Unpacking the Drama of Despair-to-Hope

Chapter Eleven

Hope as the Intractable Resolve of the Spirit

Joanna Adams

> ". . . we believe in the Holy Spirit, the Lord and Giver of
> Life . . ."
>
> The Nicene Creed

Throughout the course of its eight-week conversation, the Camp-bell Seminar scholars consistently described the nature of the context in which the church of Jesus Christ lives out its mission at the turn of the century as being marked by despair. Whether acknowledged or denied by those who are buffeted by them, the powers that work against life are formidable, unavoidable, and possessed of a tenacity that even the best intentions of individuals and social institutions can neither diminish nor defeat. Indeed, the forces of untruth, injustice, violence, banality, and nihilism are possessed of such cunning potency that ideas and actions intended for life are themselves drawn into the service of death. To state the obvious, there are other spirits besides the Spirit of God at work in the world as a new millennium dawns. This is, of course, not an unprecedented situation. It is the basic situation of the human condition, though there are potential consequences and dangers unique to our time. For example, the deteriorating condition of the global environment has brought modern civilization to the point that the very planet entrusted to our care is threatened with death."[11]

We should be careful, however, not to make too great a claim as to the exceptional nature of the current crisis of hope, for so it was in the days of old, when, from age to age, people and the systems they created turned from God, "leaving sin and death to reign."[12] Nevertheless, the current crisis is real, alarming, and distinct in that it occurs as the religious empire of Constantinian Christianity comes to a close, as Western capitalism continues its triumphant march across the world, and as the capacity for denial about the sufferings and injustices of the world deepens among the affluent and technology-advantaged.

At the same time, there is a genuine spiritual hunger loose in the world, among the advantaged as well as among the disadvantaged. It is found in the most elegant penthouses in Manhattan. It is found in the barrios of Managua. People hunger for release from oppression, boredom, and lifelessness. These malaises are sometimes the result of having too little, and sometimes the result of having too much. (I read recently about a very wealthy woman with many houses and villas who was famous among her friends for greeting visitors to any one of her residences with these words: "Welcome! It may not be home, but it's much!")[13]

It is not just spiritual hunger that is loose in the world, however. That for which the human spirit hungers is also loose in the world. At the heart of the Christian faith is the conviction that the human spirit is unsatisfied with anything short of God: "You arouse us so that praising you may bring us joy, because you have made us and drawn us to yourself, and our heart is unquiet until it rests in you."[14]

The Spirit of the triune God is and will always be the life force of the world and all that is good and hopeful in it, which includes the hunger for God.

As with every good gift that comes from God, however, human spirituality is subject to misuse, misdirection, and abuse. If, as is being predicted by most credible researchers, the twenty-first century becomes the most spiritual and religious century in the past five hundred years, then the crucial question will be how to "test the spirits to see whether they are from God" (1 John 4:1).

Surely one of the most encouraging and at the same time unsettling phenomena of our present day has been the surge of interest in spirituality of every sort. "New age" spirituality, an approach that knows little of the Christian tradition and emphasizes inner peace and self-discovery, has captured the imaginations and hearts of millions in North America. The ecclesiastical phenomenon of Pentecostalism, perhaps the fastest growing Christian movement in two thousand years, has swept across Latin America, Africa, and Asia with unprecedented power. Certainly, part of its attraction lies in its twofold emphasis on healing for physical and mental infirmities and on the promise of relief from financial woes.

What shall we make of modern spirituality, and how shall the church around the world understand its mission in relation to the

Holy Spirit at this peculiar moment in history? Certainly, each community of faith, whether it is a prayer group, a parish, a congregation, or a denomination, functions in circumstances unique to its contextual setting and historical grounding, but there are some critically important things that must be said about the work of the Spirit of God, who is "*everywhere* the giver and renewer of life."[15]

The Spirit of God is not the possession of the Christian church; neither is the Spirit at work only in and through those who claim the name of Christ. "The wind blows where it wills " (John 3:8), and, as Thomas Thangaraj reminded us, "The wind is blowing!"[16] Nevertheless, the church has always claimed a peculiar relationship to the Spirit, beginning with its origins as the creation of the Spirit at Pentecost. From the Spirit come the life and faith of the church, its capacity to discern direction for mission, its energy to act in hope.

The Spirit is the Spirit of life—from the creation of the cosmos itself, to the anointing of the prophets, to Ezekiel's dancing bones, to the conception of Jesus in the womb of a woman named Mary, to the Spirit-filled community of Pentecost, to the spread of the gospel through Asia Minor and beyond. It follows then that the church's mission must always and everywhere be to name and work against those forces that thwart and destroy life and to nurture those actions and institutions that support and honor life in all its forms. "The Holy Spirit . . . is the power that raises the dead, the power of the new creation of all things."[17]

The church can never claim to possess the power of new creation. Its own past and present have been marked by more than a little death-dealing and internal deadness. Nevertheless, the church exists in order to represent in its life and work the reality of God's death-reversing power, as accomplished in the death and resurrection of Jesus by the power of God.

Because the Spirit of God, Creator and Renewer of life, is the source of all human creativity, the church has an indispensable calling of stewardship with regard to the creative arts. The late Robert Shaw, conductor of the Atlanta Symphony and the Atlanta Symphony Chorus, issued this challenge to the church:

> If the Christian Church can accept the doctrine of "eternal life"—and most of it does—does it not follow that this life is somehow a part of that eternal one (eternity being indivisible and having no beginning and no end); and therefore, LIFE in

the universal, eternal sense—of which ours is only a very small part—must still be a becoming?

I am not arguing Genesis vs. evolution. (What's a few million years to the Infinite?) I am simply suggesting that if there is a Judeo-Christian Creator—a God of Life and Love—He/She/It somehow/somewhere/somewhen must be doing exactly that: Living and Loving.

To me it follows that the Church if it wants to keep in touch with the Creator, must provide a home for all that is—and all who are—creative, lest the church itself wither and drift into irrelevance.[18]

Because the Spirit of God is "the Spirit of truth, whom the world cannot receive, because it neither sees him nor knows him" (John 14:17), the church must attend to the mission of seeking the truth and allow itself to be led by the Spirit into truth, as revealed in Jesus of Nazareth and as testified to by the scriptures of the Old and New Testaments. In an era in which many in the church are drawn to emotion and ecstatic experience as verifications for the presence of the Holy Spirit, it is crucial to remember that God is at work in thought as well as feeling. In an age in which intellectual pursuits are increasingly dismissed as irrelevant to authentic spirituality, it is essential that the church be a center for moral and theological discourse and for the search for wisdom in every area of life.

The Spirit of God does not lead the church into a false spirituality that is otherworldly and immaterial but into flesh and blood witness to the God whose will is salvation for all people but especially the lowly and the oppressed. Indeed, what we do materially is itself deeply spiritual. Jesus himself was appointed, sent, and empowered by the Spirit in this mission: "The Spirit of the Lord is upon me, because he has anointed me to bring good news to the poor. He has sent me to proclaim release to the captives and recovery of sight to the blind, to let the oppressed go free, to proclaim the year of the Lord's favor" (Luke 4:18–19). This-worldliness on the church's part, in the sense of advocacy for those who are forgotten or excluded by society and for those bound by chains of injustice, is the mark of authentic life in the Spirit.

Two additional points need to be made here:

1. We can be sure that wherever the work of justice, freedom, and enlightenment is being done, the initiative for the work and the power

for the work come from the Spirit. Wherever people bravely bear witness to the truth, whenever people lay down their lives for one another, there the Spirit of God is operative. The church can give thanks that God's mission is not dependent upon the faithfulness to the cause of Christ by those who claim to follow him.

2. God's realm is not in any way confined to the church. The world is the realm of God, who, as Holy Spirit, is inspiring and empowering wherever the Spirit sees fit. In other words, the Spirit is at work through, outside, and sometimes in spite of the church. The realistic acceptance of this all-too-evident truth need not be a cause for despair or inaction. Instead, it might serve to save the church from the ever-present dangers of grandiosity and pride. It might also lead to the liberating and encouraging realization that, because God is not in the position of needing Christians to accomplish the ends to which God is committed, the efforts of the Christians can become imbued with new energy, born of gratitude, to bear witness to that which God has accomplished in Jesus Christ. Just as there is no warrant for self-congratulation, there is no reason to fear failure.

The Letter to the Romans tells us that we are being "led by the Spirit of God" into our true identity as "children of God" (8:14). What is crucial to note here is the pronoun "we." The journey toward our true identity is not a solo spiritual pilgrimage. The Spirit leads us in community toward an inheritance that is to be received alongside our sisters and brothers in the family of God. What is equally striking is Paul's use of verb tenses. While we are waiting for our adoption, that adoption has, in a very real sense, already taken place. The implications for mission are clear: If we are joint heirs, we ought to act like it and stop living as if the categories of class, race, nationality, and religion are of any ultimate importance. Moreover, mutuality, not individuality, lies at the heart of the Christian promise for this world and the world to come. A church that preaches individual salvation alone will be in a far country, a great distance from the future God intends to give.

The hope of the world and therefore of the church cannot be grounded in any notion of human progress and certainly not in any expectation about the present or future effectiveness of the church. In my own denomination, anxiety about the future is pervasive and debilitating and a revealing sign that mainline American Presbyterians have perhaps grounded their hope more in a particular theological tradition and ecclesiastical structure than in "the mighty activity of the Holy Spirit."[19] In our age, as in every age that has preceded it, God's mission has a future; indeed, God's mission is the future.

In the challenging arena of religious pluralism, which is now and certainly in the twenty-first century will be one of the defining realities, a renewed emphasis on the Third Person of the Trinity offers new possibilities for thought and action. Columbia Seminary's George Stroup suggests that:

> When Christians encounter the realities of new life in the midst of death, hope in the midst of hopelessness, and movements toward justice and reconciliation in the midst of grinding oppression, it may be that the appropriate question is not whether these developments are to be understood in terms of the hidden presence of Jesus Christ but whether they are the work of the Spirit of the Triune God, the same Spirit who sends and is sent by Jesus. . . . When Christians encounter vitality, truth and justice in their pluralistic world, the first issue may not be baptism but doxology.[20]

In mission, the question has less to do with whether Jesus is named and more to do with whether the purposes of the Living God, whom Christians know through Christ, are being served.

The twenty-first century church must not lose its commitment to witness to the death-defeating, transforming power of the Spirit of God in the lives of individuals, as well as in the church, the broader realms of society, and in the created order. Behind the phenomenon of the dramatic growth of evangelicalism and Pentecostalism around the globe lie a number of causes. Some of those causes need to be vigorously tested and challenged, particularly when primary emphasis is placed upon other-worldly enthusiasm, self-improvement, or personal aggrandizement. The point of authentication for every movement that claims to be grounded in Jesus Christ is found in Jesus Christ and nowhere else. Who was he, and what did he do? What did the Spirit lead him to say and do? With whom did he break bread? Whom did he welcome? Whose tables did he overturn? Where and how, then, are we most likely to encounter his living Spirit now? The function of the Spirit is not now and never has been to give us what we want or to whisk us away from "this wretched, wretched world;" it is to fit us for life and witness in this world, for which the Son of God lived and died.

All of that said, however, central to the Christian message has always been the possibility of conversion through Word and Holy

Spirit, the gift of faith, and a transformed human spirit. Of course, neither the church nor an individual possesses the Spirit in any sense. Both are possessed by the Spirit and blessed with spiritual gifts to be employed to the glory of God and for the well-being of the community and the world.

If some Pentecostals and evangelicals overemphasize conversion and the bestowal of spiritual gifts, other Christians often tend to ignore them. Surely, it is a crucially important responsibility for the church in our day to reclaim the promise of new life for the individual, of new life in relationship to others, made possible by the power of God. The traditional names for these concerns are "conversion" and "sanctification."

Columbia Professor of Reformed Theology Shirley Guthrie helpfully frames the issue in this way:

> How do we come to say not only God and Father, but **my** God and Father; not only Lord, but **our** Lord. How does what God did "back there" touch **us** and affect our lives? These questions become the central theme as we begin to speak of the work of God the Holy Spirit.[21]

Abroad in every land is deep concern about family life, about drug and alcohol abuse, about personal character and responsibility. Raising children to be good human beings who love God and neighbor has never been a more daunting task than now, when material success and personal fulfillment have become for many the goal and purpose of human existence. Whatever else the Christian faith has maintained, it has always wanted to affirm that the Spirit of the Living God has made possible a more excellent way of life than that of the surrounding society. And besides, our hope for salvation, although it is not confined to ourselves, at the very least ought to include ourselves. It has been suggested that there is

> a double focus and goal of Christian spirituality: a vertical focus—the continual transformation into the likeness of Jesus, the resurrected Lord; and a horizontal focus—the following of Jesus in similar obedience of the Father's missional calling. . . . Both of these foci and goals can only be carried out in the power of the Spirit and undergirded by God's love.[22]

Because the New Testament church was led by the Spirit to move beyond the parameters set by the religious establishment as to who was

acceptable and who was unacceptable in the eyes of God, so the church
of the twenty-first century needs to be open to moving beyond some
of its present assumptions. The Spirit of God is free to include
whomever the Spirit wants in the promises of salvation. There are
habits of the Spirit that have been historically consistent, such as the
habit of opening doors instead of closing them. There is also the matter of Christian vocation and the challenge that many women around
the world face as they are categorically excluded from answering God's
call to ministry in the church. Perhaps one of the central texts for our
time might be: "Then afterward I will pour out my Spirit on all flesh;
your sons *and* your daughters shall prophesy" (Joel 2:28, my emphasis).

The Apostles' Creed offers the church of Jesus Christ a hopeful set
of expectations as to what we have every right to hope for in the future
that is even now unfolding: "I believe in the Holy Ghost; the holy
catholic church, the forgiveness of sins, the resurrection of the body;
and the life everlasting." When we make these affirmations as a body
of believers, we are saying at least these things:

1. The presence and power of God is real and present and can never
be deterred from the mission of God, which is to turn the whole of
the created order into the new heaven and the new earth. The universe and everyone in it are being drawn toward the peace and justice,
the love and well-being, that are at the core of God's will for all.

2. Because the church is holy, the church belongs to God, and God
will finally determine its membership, its mission, and its destiny.
Because it is catholic, it is found in all nations. Therefore, we will
never put our ultimate trust in our own church and its special take on
things. We will listen to voices other than our own. We will not make
an idol of our own experience, whatever that experience might be.

3. Because the Spirit offers the gift of communion with Christ, we
are therefore blessed with the gift of communion with one another,
through the one in whom all things in heaven and on earth hold
together (Col. 1:16–17). There is no power on earth that is equal to
the power of the love of God as revealed in the sacrifice and death of
Jesus, Son of God, on the cross. In the cross alone rest our hope and
our strength. And who can conceive of a more countercultural concept than that of a community that gathers around a table at which a
broken body is served and hears the astonishing claim that "every time
you eat this bread . . . you proclaim the saving death of the risen Lord
until he comes" (1 Cor. 11:26)?

4. Because we believe in the forgiveness of sins, we are obliged to

forgive one another. Is this not the most radical work of the Holy Spirit, this work of forgiveness and reconciliation for which the world is so desperately hungry? If God forgives our sins, then we have no ground on which to stand when we rigidly judge and self-righteously condemn others. The implications are profound, as members of churches in the those parts of the world that have suffered the ill effects of attempts to "Christianize the unsaved," whatever the cost, create new relationships with those whose ancestors were committed to such a mission. It also challenges the church in every place to let go of any attitude of superiority and to assume the posture of humble gratitude in relation to God and to others.

5. When we say that we believe in the resurrection of the body, we are not only affirming our trust in the power of God over the forces of death, but also acknowledging that death itself is real and inevitable. This honest acknowledgment saves us from the naive expectation that invincibility is possible for human beings or for the empires they create. More important, it affirms that beyond the worst that death and the forces of destruction can do is the best that God can do, and what God can do—indeed, has already done—will forever be more than enough. It teaches the church to rest its hope, not in good mission strategies or the expectation of escape from a world drawn daily toward despair. It teaches us to ground our hope in the new reality created by the death and resurrection of Jesus from the dead. Like all other institutions, the church breathes in the toxins of hopelessness minute by minute, but the church has, at its best, always lived out of its conviction that the new creation has begun, and it has been able to see signs of its coming, even in the most desperate situations. It has maintained that God came nearest to us in a unique act of self-giving love and that when we ourselves engage in similar actions we are most likely to encounter the presence of the Living God, the Spirit of the Risen Christ.

Above all else, the mission of the church depends upon its capacity to receive the spiritual gifts of hope, courage, and imagination. The words of the *Brief Statement of Faith* (PCUSA) capture the essence of the hope into which we are to live as a new century unfolds:

> In gratitude to God, empowered by the Spirit, we strive to serve Christ in our daily tasks and to live holy and joyful lives, even as we watch for God's new heaven and new earth, praying, "Come, Lord Jesus!"

Chapter Twelve

Hope as the Coming Reign of God

H. Russel Botman

> No one can pray for the kingdom . . . who thinks up a king-
> dom for himself [*sic*] . . . who lives for his own world view
> and knows a thousand programs and prescriptions by which
> he would like to cure the world . . ."
> Dietrich Bonhoeffer, *Thy Kingdom Come*
> (Philadelphia: Fortress, 1979), 34

How shall we speak of hope in the twenty-first century? How can such a term have meaning in a world where human beings have outsmarted themselves and have reached the point where they speak of the "end of history"? This chapter examines the notion of "hope" as a category of grace and not of nature. What does it imply, and how are we to theologically articulate it in the twenty-first century? I take my theological point of departure in the notion of the reign of God, which bears the double dimension of the "already" and the "not yet."

"Hope" Against Hope

The members of the Campbell Seminar share the conviction that hope is an adequate redemptive category for mission in the twenty-first century or a healing metaphor for future generations. We share a certain criticism of a missionary endeavor in this world that is essentially an expression of otherworldliness. Otherworldly mission cannot but deny the biblical connection between the Creator and creation, because it sequentially divorces the future of creation from the future of its Creator. In this "otherworldly" way, "hope," the necessary precondition to any yearning for "future," is destroyed already in the here and now. Incrementally, such undoing leads to worldwide despair.

The world is accustomed to despair. It has known personal despair, familial despair, national and regional despair. This time, however, the world and all its religions are faced with an unprecedented crisis of global despair. But then again, even "global" despair is not unfamiliar to the peoples of the world. Global despair has already shaken the foundations of hope in two well-documented and horrific world wars. The major difference of the current crisis of hope is that it rears its head at a time when the world is experiencing its optimal political (e.g., the end of the Cold War and an unprecedented embrace of democracy), economic (e.g., the flourishing financial market), technological (e.g., the growth of the Internet), and cultural (e.g., the embrace of diversity) moment in history. As every category of the global graph is pointing upward, the graph of human hope has plummeted and continues to do so in all sectors of human stratification. This "unprecedented crisis of hope" represents the crux of the missional challenge of the twenty-first century.

Then again, the world is not unfamiliar with hope. Colonial expansion and its parallel mission of Livingstone's type, and later the cultural Americanization of the world and its parallel mission based on American televangelism, have in the past and continue to prophesy their own version of hope to all nations and to the ends of the world. This kind of mission, with its questionable articulation of Christian hope, must be transformed for the sake of future generations.

It is also necessary to be careful not to search for hope based on despair. It is not a struggle to make sense of the decay, the depression, and the despair that will bring us to an adequate understanding of hope for the twenty-first century. We must conduct proper analysis of the context[23] and come to an in-depth understanding of the nature of despair.[24] Nothing in us, nothing of us, or of this world, not even its suffering and despair, can bring us to an understanding of the real depth of Christian hope.

Confessing hope in action requires a theological grounding to become meaningful in the twenty-first century. The notion of the reign of God has often been invoked in times of deep crisis and despair in the world.[25]

The Unmaking of a Historical-Deterministic Hope

The Constantinian state and its triumphal church were seen not only as signs of the reign of God but also as the ultimate expression of it. Both church and state enjoyed a continuous relationship with the central mission and gift to Christian discipleship, namely, the reign of God.

Modernity was later born of the enthusiasm of a certain messianic hope expressed in terms of nature and the theology of "the orders of creation." The people of the Enlightenment believed that (a) nature will eventually complete its own course, (b) the world will on its own develop to autonomy and maturity, (c) education will progressively lead to humanization and the fruits of democratization and civilization, (d) history was essentially open to the future of its natural completion.

The Renaissance turned the human being into "the measure of all things" and placed it under the leadership of the European. The instrumentalization of reason (rationality) of this central (European) human being (anthropology) became the basis of a (natural) hope for a complete and matured future of every person and place in the world (especially for the so-called proletariat). Under the leadership of this European subject, rationality became the instrument of domination. This led to a colonial seizure of power over "poorer peoples of the land" who lived in the so-called new worlds "discovered" by the Europeans (leading to large-scale political dehumanization of "the other"), a technological seizure of power over the environment (leading to cosmic ecological destruction), and a continued march to economic domination over all the excluded peoples (leading to a this-worldly sacrifice in the global economy). This enthusiastic, European messianic hope, with its strong claim that human beings can achieve the world's fulfillment through rational means, and its resultant technological achievements robbed human beings of their ecology (expressed through its intra- and extra-relationships) and the environment of its magic (expressed as divine mystery). This hopeful enthusiasm deprived both humanity and the environment of their authentic being as it was given in their relationship to the Creator.

Assisted by ancient and modern theological approaches to nature and the theology of the "orders of creation," this Christian European domination also resulted in genocide, world wars, the massive oppression and enslavement of African people, and the brutal conquest of many parts and peoples of the world, and also of the environment.

The beliefs of modernity were rooted in religious ideas: for instance, sixteenth-century apocalyptic thought, messianism in the time of the resettlement of Jews, the identification of England with the lost tribes of Israel and its messianic myth, German pietism, Puritan apocalypticism, the idea of a chosen people in the politics of apartheid, and millenarianism. The idea that the former millennium would be the golden age was directly related to the notion of it as being the Christian age. Ever since the year 1097 C.E. and into the years immediately after 1400 C.E., Christians planned, sought, and organized military missions to take Jerusalem from the Muslims. Having sacrificed the lives of many Christian and Muslim children in the crusades, Christians, thereafter, shifted their missionary focus toward the so-called new worlds. Mission was extended from Jerusalem to the ends of the earth (Acts 1:8).

Hope, an important category of redemption, has thus been expressed (co-opted) for many centuries as the expression of a rational evolution of nature led by human beings, albeit through domination and subjugation of others.

The unmaking of actions of hope manifested as development of nature requires at the end of the twentieth century a conceptual break from progress-faith; instrumental rationality; Constantinian, colonial, and every form of empire Christendom; an ecumenical movement embedded in Christendom; and even a Christian European civilization embedded in the Southern Hemisphere.

The unmaking of hope has a long history, but recent history has both accelerated and reshaped the process. If people are asked when last they have heard the song "We shall overcome, we shall overcome someday, for deep in my heart I do believe that we shall overcome someday," not in a movie of the 1960s but on the streets where Christianity has always been called to confess its hope, most will say in the late sixties, some will say in the seventies, fewer will say in the eighties, and perhaps only a handful might say in the nineties. This is the condition of the world, almost in every corner of its geography, as we enter the twenty-first century. This reality tells its own story. The plummeting of the graph of social hope did not start in 1990, when Mandela was released, or in 1989, when the Berlin wall came down. Global hopelessness started when Nelson Mandela was sentenced to lifelong imprisonment, when black people were first massacred in Sharpeville (South Africa), when the armies of the Warsaw Pact undermined the humane nature of socialism, when Martin Luther King Jr. was murdered, when Vietnam erupted, when modern terrorism showed its face, and when economic globalization graduated from a mere posture of internationalization to growing global inequality. The unmaking of social hope has continued ever since the 1960s to the very day when we are now called to confess hope in action.

Reawakening to Christian Hope

The unmaking of hope deepened in the 1970s to such a level that the ecumenical movement awakened to its alternative. The Fifth Assembly of the World Council of Churches met in Nairobi, Kenya, November 23 to December 10, 1975. The theme of the assembly was "Jesus Christ Frees and Unites." It is not only the time but also the place of the meeting that is significant from the perspective of mission. Section I of the assembly had the responsibility to develop the subtheme "Confessing Christ Today." An extraordinary level of convergence occurred among the four major traditions of the council as the report took shape. At the heart of this convergence was the assertion that the missionary witness of the time should be grounded in the confession of Christ as "the Christ of God, the hope of the world." The second landmark event that testifies to the reawakening to hope is the 1978 meeting of the Faith and Order Commission of the World Council of Churches in Bangalore, India. Again, both time and place are of significance. This meeting studied the implications of hope as they see Christians called to "give account of the hope" that is in them. They developed the overarching idea of "hope as the resistance movement against fatalism." It took the ecumenical movement a decade to theologically respond in the light of the new, accelerated forms of the unmaking of hope. The third ecumenical landmark is the 1998 Assembly of the World Council of Churches in Harare, Zimbabwe, which met under the theme "Turn to God: Rejoice in Hope." The significance of time and place speaks for itself. The Campbell Seminar of Columbia Theological Seminary, meeting from September 18 to November 10, 2000, stands in this tradition and breaks with the usual pattern of place, while honoring the ecumenical and interdisciplinary nature of the challenge for mission in the twenty-first century. Again, date and (new) place have great significance.

Standing at the beginning of the twenty-first century, the cries for hope rise above the global horizon. Economic globalization represents unprecedented wealth in small pockets of the world and unprecedented despair "unto the ends of the earth." Can we remake hope from the ravages of the Enlightenment and its accelerated forms of the 1960s? No, we can't! We can, perhaps, make "false hope" from these constructs, but real hope that will save our world and its people will have to be rooted in eschatology and received as a gift of grace.

Jesus' response to a society seeking hope (the extent of which is articulated by the many references to "the crowds," "the multitude," and the "city of Jerusalem," and the single reference to the couple walking home after the crucifixion to a town called Emmaus) was manifested in the announcement of the "coming of the reign of God." This claim to hope represents for the people of early Palestine, as for us today, the most crucial break with natural expectations. It logically refers to the waves of the future breaking on the beaches of the here and now of our despair. We can, therefore, look at the kind of world we live in without abdicating to the despair or false hope we ourselves (and our ancestors) have constructed (naturally). The world can now be called to hope against all natural hope.

The twenty-first century calls Christians to remake the Christian hope by basing it anew in the new acts that God is doing in the world today. This eschatological hope does not start with Jesus. It is foundational to the whole revelation of the triune God. The Bible reveals God acting in history.[26] Such hope must be expressed as a category of grace, not of nature. Its existence is a gift of grace; its revelation, a mystery of grace; and its historical appearance, a manifestation of grace. The redemptive category of hope thus breaks with the modern logic of cause and effect in all matters of nature. At this point, the hope Christians are called to confess in the twenty-first century differs radically from the hope manifested in the deterministic understandings of Marxism, modern capitalism, and the Enlightenment.

Mission as Hope in Action

David Bosch neatly indicates that "it should come as no surprise that the recovery of the eschatological dimension is manifested particularly clearly in missionary circles."[27] He continues, "From the very beginning of the Christian church there appeared to have been a peculiar affinity between the missionary enterprise and expectations of a fundamental change in the future of humankind. . . . Eschatology stands for the hope element in religion."[28] Hope, I would say, represents the eschatological-historical character of Christian faith. Faith is being, historically, sure of what we hope for in that we are certain of what we do not see as a result of the "not yet" character of eschatology (Heb. 11:1). However, at the dawn of the twenty-first century, we can be sure that the "already" of God's reign outweighs the "not yet" (to use Oscar Cullmann's expression) of its eschatology.

David Bosch's most direct critique of the theology and mission of apartheid is rooted in Oscar Cullmann's point about the direct relationship between mission and eschatology. Although the Dutch Reformed Church states in its document "Church and Society" (1990) that it has done everything in service of the reign of God, Bosch remarks that "if . . . their refusal to challenge unjust societal structures is rooted in a view about the inviolability of the 'orders of creation,' they cannot appeal to . . . Cullmann."[29] There is a certain platitude in the language of the reign of God, even when used by zealous missionaries, when such a notion is embedded in ideas about the "orders of creation" and is thereby separated from the critical element of eschatology.

After the dismantling of apartheid and the fall of the Berlin Wall, an adulterated eschatology has arisen whereby some look at the ravages of history, the destruction of nature, the AIDS epidemic, and ongoing conflicts as signs of the Parousia that indicate the nearness of the "coming reign of God." The faithful should now prepare to meet the "King." This is not the first time that eschatology has been used to justify apathy. The category of hope has itself often led to quietism, passivity, and paralysis. The gift of God becomes something that one should wait for. One is then challenged to be patient and willing to endure suffering until it comes to pass. In such situations, hope functions as a narcotic of the people. We therefore have to ask whether there is a relationship between hope and action. Indeed, the relationship is found in the Christian's calling to discipleship. The purport of Christianity is not that we follow Descartes, Plato, Martin Luther King Jr., or Desmond Mpilo Tutu but that Christians shall follow Christ. The mission of the triune God calls for action in terms of the *imitatio Dei* (the following of God). It is God's mission, and every action of human beings can be only a following. Confessing hope is confession and not acts of human assertiveness. The hope of a disciple is never based on one's own agency but on one's following of the acting God who has acted then in Jesus Christ and now in and among us all in the world.

Such remaking should therefore lead to a clearer understanding of hope in action. There is a vast difference between Bosch's proposal for mission as "action in hope" and the idea of confessing as proposed here. Building on H. J. Margull's viewpoints, Bosch chooses to speak of "action in hope." Bosch then makes his definitive statement: "We perform this mission in hope." Although he qualifies this definitive statement with the words "with due humility—as participation in the missio Dei," I find it still too restricted to acting in anticipation of what lies in the future. It elevates the action to an eschatology of expectation rather than one of God's action here and now. Eventually, this line of thought falls prey to a surplus of the future and a deficit of the here and now. He can therefore state that "it may be correct to label our entire, comprehensive mission in the context of our eschatological expectation as 'action in hope.'"[30] We are not merely called to act in anticipatory hope. Our mission in the twenty-first century is to confess hope in action following God's actions in our times. We take our point of departure in the notion that God is acting in history, at this time, in this place, in this country, and in this world. Our mission is to confess this hope. However, confessing this hope passively is not a following of God in this world. We are called to confess hope in action.

Is hope in action "a defensible decision of faith"? Does it not represent the dangers of a justification by works? Discipleship cannot be a category of justification by works, for it is a category of sanctification. Indeed, insofar as this hope is understood as an action that is (a) based on the new actions of God in history, (b) rooted in the promises of God, (c) a conscious break from the frame of a natural or social causality, (d) a critical challenge to Christianity and the church in the world, and (e) a call to embodiment, it is an *imitatio Dei.*

Hope's final and most decisive basis lies in the idea that the prophetic action, the priestly death, and the reigning resurrection of Christ welcomed the reign of God into this world and continues to sustain it. We may not know precisely what the things of the end will be like, but we do know that when all human and natural resources for hope have been defeated, then hope, arising from God, shall not evaporate, because God is doing new things among us. We have tried living with a form of "hope" that comes from our achievements, but we are now challenged by a hope that comes from outside the realm of the human and the natural.

In the stark reality of the death of Christ, we meet the terrible hopelessness that entrapped the disciples. The cross is the end of their history. The cross is the end of their Christianity and, yes, of their hopes for humanity. The cross represents the end of their mission. In a sense, the cross of Christ is our most real exposure to the meaning of the words *end, fear,* and *hopelessness.* In the cross, we meet the limits of all being and doing, the final defeat of hope in the world, in people, and in the finest institutions of religion, law, and government. All that is left is to return home and wait for the bubble to burst (Luke 24:13–24).

Christians have, for too many years, been interpreting the cross one-sidedly in an Anselmic way so that we see only the doctrine of satisfaction in it. We see this man, Jesus Christ, and those people who crucified him as puppets on the string of an avenging God who has chosen the cross for God's own satisfaction. Satisfied that all sins were atoned for, this God then performs another miracle: the resurrection of Christ. However, we never got the point made by the Gospel of Mark.[31] The cross left the most ardent believer without hope, silenced, and afraid (Mark 16:8). With these descriptions, Mark concludes his writing. Awkward as that may be, Mark's original conclusion is the most instructive conclusion for people facing the realities of the twenty-first century. As we are facing the end of human development,[32] the end of history, and the end of evolution, we are standing where those disciples stood: facing the cross. We are used to seeing cross-bearers in our families and in poor countries. We have not yet learned the deep meaninglessness, and hopelessness that come with the cross. We are now called back to the cross of Christ to ask again for its reason as we think about the church's mission in the twenty-first century. Perhaps, this time we will be struck by the true meaning of its futurelessness and hopelessness. Only then will we be able to understand the meaning of resurrection. At the height of hopelessness, an act of hope that comes not from us, that has not been developed through human rationality, that bears no relation to evolution, and that has never been seen before surprises hopeless people. As an act of God, coming from outside everything we are, know, and have, the resurrection of Jesus Christ brings hope also for the twenty-first century. Here and now, in a graceless, hopeless, and brutal world, the light of grace breaks the darkness of hopelessness.

The reference to the cross of Jesus Christ must not be seen, here, as a legal recall to historical precedence. Walter Brueggemann has reminded us of von Rad's powerful assertion of the theological implications of the words of the exilic prophet: "Do not remember the former things. I am about to do a new thing" (Isa. 43:18–19). This prophetic statement, he says, hinges on the sociopolitical and religious crises of the exile in the year 587 B.C.E. in Jerusalem. The known world of the Israelites had its final crash. They reached the end of all known categories. At such a time, Brueggemann suggests, the world needs prophetic imagination. Only prophetic imagination will be able to look for and see the new acts of God in this world, here and now.[33]

How should we understand this call not to remember former things in the light of mission in the twenty-first century? The reference to "former things" does not refer to human actions. Although we know that the Babylonians had asserted their power politically and militarily in the interests of the empire, the exilic prophets insisted on a theological explanation, which entails that the judgment of God has sent them into exile. Well aware of this interpretation, God now says, "Do not remember former things." God thereby suggests that they would do well not to look for precedence in natural law or even divine intervention. It means that God is doing a thing that is new even unto God. Realistically, deep-seated hope lies in the prophetic imagination that the "newness" of God's action will be without any historical (human and/or divine) or legal (natural or tradition-based) precedence. Instead, we are invited to imagine the future by seeing new, surprising divine acts in this-worldly history.[34] We are now challenged to embrace the ideas of future and hope beyond the end of a mere belief in the natural unfolding of a created order or a technological climax of reason. Beyond that, we are even challenged to see hope beyond a divine form of historical precedence. Real faithful embrace of hope does not arise from the ashes of a natural theology or from divine historical precedence but from the awakening to a hope for a future that is manifested in the very idea that God has a future.

God's future is inseparable from the future of every single being in God's creation and also from every single historical judgment of God with regard to this world. This is the plain and simple meaning of hope at the end of history. God does not want and did not plan on having a future separate from or without creation. The act of the resurrection and the promise of the *basilea* (reign) of God mean, beyond all doubt, that God has chosen this world as the theater of God's grace. It is not just happenstance that Jesus used parables of this world to explain to us the meaning of the reign of God. The reign of God is so tied up with nature that it bears the elements of graceful and prophetic imagination in itself. Although the parables of the reign of God are brought to us through the mediation of the metaphors of nature, there is no single point in which nature contributes to its making. The stories about the reign of God talk about the actions of human beings (e.g., the merciful Samaritan) and the processes of nature (e.g., the growth of the mustard seed), but never do they so much as hint at a human or evolutionary contribution to the coming of the reign of God. This world and its people can only receive it.

Focusing this hope on the new acts of God does not imply a sacrifice of reason. This is the mistaken perception of discipleship that continues to dominate the theological perceptions of many scholars in history. Dietrich Bonhoeffer's well-known statement that "when Christ calls a man, he calls him 'come and die,'" is totally misunderstood by people who think that Bonhoeffer promoted a Christianity that sacrifices reason. Nobody who worked with the concept of discipleship was more critical and thought provoking than Bonhoeffer.

Nevertheless, discipleship necessitates a hermeneutical readjustment to the sites of the poor and the marginalized in the world. The new acts that God is doing among us are happening as acts of liberation and humanization, not only as new acts but also in the unexpected places. Only the naive fail to see the socioeconomic power of this substantial, this-worldly hope for the twenty-first century. However, we are called into this hope by way of a form of knowing embedded in the suspension of a socially acquired interpreting framework of an advantageous socioeconomic status. Remaking Christian hope requires specific attention to the poor and marginalized people of the Southern Hemisphere (Africa, Asia, the Caribbean, Latin America) and its diaspora in the north.

Future leadership in Christianity will have to come from the Southern Hemisphere as the number of Christians continues to grow in these regions. As an African, it means to me that African Christianity shares two characteristics with the early church: it has its own forms of pre-Constantinian suffering and shares economic exclusion with the poor communities of the early church, which looked to rich converts for its own mission. Hope in action includes investment in religious leadership, theological education, and projects that confess hope in action in the Southern Hemisphere and, also, its diaspora living in the north.[35] The remaking of Christian hope in the twenty-first century beckons the West to a new commitment, to a new generosity in mission, and to human development.

It also challenges Christians in the Southern Hemisphere to take responsibility for enacting social hope by confessing hope in action. This means, in the face of fear, "confess hope in action"; confronted by poverty, "confess hope in action"; facing the scourge of AIDS, "confess hope in action"!

The global economic world includes the exclusion of specified people in an economic reality that requires their (unfortunate, but) necessary sacrifice (triage) in a world of limits. However, some parts of the gospel message claim that if any Christian should give up hope for any one (even the smallest) of the creatures of God (whether it is a child or an orchid), that person has abandoned all hope for the future of God as Creator. Such hopelessness is a faithlessness that constitutes godlessness. The pursuit of Christian hope in an era of global despair rests not so much on the natural potential of nature as on the potent commitment and faithfulness of the Creator to the works (creation) of God's hands.

Conclusion: Idealism for Some, Redemption for Others?

As Christians enter the twenty-first century, we will do well to confess our complicity in the making of worldwide despair. Then we shall do better by confessing, without blinking an eye, hope in action. We will find that God is using others also in this great mission. We shall rejoice when we see them, knowing that we are facing an unprecedented crisis in world history in which we all need acts of grace.

When the scientist works with conscience to find a cure for cancer, we see God's mission as hope in action. When people call for the forgiveness of the debt of "the third world countries," we see God's mission as hope in action. When an investor in North America conducts business as if the children in Africa are his or her own, we see God's mission as hope in action. When a Cuban doctor goes to the poor villages of South Africa to reduce the infant mortality rate, we see God's mission as hope in action. When a person in sub-Saharan Africa is trained to care for people living with HIV-AIDS, we see God's mission as hope in action. When a church opens its heart to the homeless, we see God's mission as hope in action. When subjugated cultures find their way back into the church, we see God's mission as hope in action. When communities opt for reconciliation instead of civil war, we see God's mission as hope in action. When Columbia Theological Seminary invests in research for mission by all in the world, scholars from different contexts see God's mission as hope in action. When Walter Brueggemann writes about the painful issues of the land, Africans see God's mission as hope in action. I know you want to stop me here, saying, "But these things are already happening." I answer, "Precisely, my argument as well!"

I could imagine further that the day will dawn, as Christians continue their own missional confession, when millions will demand, as they must, in the face of overwhelming hope in action and by the inspiration of the Holy Spirit, "Tell us the reason for your hope." We shall tell them the story of God acting in history and what it meant to us. I can imagine them listening, astounded by the story that our hope is rooted in grace and not in nature. I imagine them turning their eyes to their healing bodies, to their changing societies, to their reconciled communities, to their newfound friendships, and I imagine them saying: "Amen. Come Lord Jesus" (Rev. 22:20).

This is the mystery of confessing hope in action. The deed and the word become one by the grace of God and no longer by nature.

Biblical hope remains the neglected mission of God as the church, adamantly, professes the missiological primacy of "faith" and "love" over "hope" in the triad of 1 Corinthians 13 as if the three can be separated. Will teachers of mission and theology be diligent enough to form students and pastors critical enough to engage the neglected mission of the church at this critical juncture in the history of humanity and the earth?

Chapter Thirteen

Despair as Pervasive Ailment

Douglas John Hall

The Question

The only fundamental reason for articulating Christian mission as hope in action is that we discern in our field of mission—today's global society—a pervasive loss, diminution, or distortion of hope. Were we to read the signs of our times in other ways (for example, as manifesting rampant chaos, debilitating guilt, or crippling fear), we would have to express our mission as Christians in different terms (providential order, divine forgiveness, trust). Whatever has the prospect of becoming "gospel" must address the reality of the negating condition lying at the heart of the situation concerned. Gospel is *good* news because and as it engages, challenges, resolves, or ameliorates the *bad* news actually present in the sphere of missiological concern. A gospel that spoke to the human anxiety of "guilt and condemnation" when the dominant anxiety of its context is more nearly "meaninglessness and despair" (Tillich) would not be gospel; indeed, it would probably function repressively to distract the attention of its hearers away from their existential anxiety.

In one way or another, all of our discussions in the seminar have mentioned—and some of us have accentuated—the deprivation of hope as the spiritual hallmark of the present and impending global future. Such an analysis is corroborated by the reflections of many observers of our era, including the Roman Catholic thinker Raimon Panikkar, who in a recent article proposed an interfaith council to address the "crisis of humanity":

> The crisis today is not that of one country, one model, one regime; it is a crisis of humanity. . . . Three quarters of the world's population live under inhuman conditions. Humanity is in such

great distress and insecurity that its leaders believe they must keep 30 million men in arms! The church cannot be a stranger to such distress, to such institutionalized injustice. It cannot remain deaf to the cries of the people, especially of the humble and the poor. The council I would propose would certainly not be exclusively Christian but ecumenical, in the sense that it would give a hearing to other cosmologies and religions. Its purpose would be to determine how the Spirit is inspiring humanity to live in peace, and to bear *the joyous news of hope.*[36]

Another recent article brings the discussion nearer home:

> Our hopes are a measure of our greatness. When they shrink, we ourselves are diminished. The story of American hope over the past two centuries is one of increasing narrowing . . . the horizon of hope has shrunk to "the scale of self-pampering."[37]

Innumerable other testimonies to the loss of hope could be cited—some religious, some secular. We may count, therefore, on a great deal of backing when we make this approach our own. But words are important, and the question that I want to address in this paper is whether *despair* is an appropriate category into which to translate the diminishment or distortion of hope that we sense. I alluded earlier to two of the three "dominant forms of anxiety" identified by Paul Tillich as characteristic of human existence under the conditions of the Fall. Tillich believed that all three types ("fate and death," dominant in the classical period; "guilt and condemnation," dominant in the medieval period; and "meaninglessness and despair") are always present but that historical epochs manifest the predominance of one type. Overwhelmingly, he insisted, the dominant anxiety of our present age is the third type. Along with many others, I have pursued that same analysis in my own work. For the most part, however, Christians in the West are still drawing upon the medieval and Reformation assumption that the human predicament is one of "guilt and condemnation." The prevailing soteriologies of Western Christendom, both Catholic and Protestant, continue to rely heavily on Anselm's satisfaction theory of atonement, which is addressed precisely to that anxiety. That this is so relates to the earlier observation that religion frequently represses the disturbing consciousness of present reality by concentrating on the reality of the past—which in any case is always easier to deal with! Failure to address the anxiety of "meaninglessness and despair" is also, and more deeply, due to the fact that of all the forms of human anxiety it is the most excruciating to contemplate and the most difficult to engage from the side of gospel.

There is still another reason why, in "developed" societies especially, the judgment that the human condition is one of "meaninglessness and despair" is difficult to entertain. Successful peoples are likely to find such language exaggerated. They may be willing to have it applied to individuals or to specific groupings ("the urban poor," "racial minorities," "the young"), but as a characterization of the spiritual condition of their culture at large (as in the Volf quotation) such bleak language seems inappropriate, if not ridiculous.

If, therefore, we intend such a reading of our planetary context to be heard also (perhaps even especially!) in such societies, we shall have to parse the term *despair* in a very careful and sensitive manner. To suggest that the entire world is wrapped in a garment of deep and obvious gloom would be to invite ridicule. There are happy and cheerful persons everywhere, and only a confirmed pessimist could fail to admit the reality of ordinary human expectancy that shines through in the public arena, despite the horrors and negativities held up to us hourly by the news industry. Our discussion of the global context in terms of "despair" will be credible only if we can delve more deeply into its reality as a *spiritual condition* informing planetary existence in ways not easily discerned or immediately visible.

Overt and Covert Despair

The word *despair* means literally the negation of hope (*de* + *sperare*, fr. *spes* [hope]). Because life itself depends upon the will to face the future with some degree of sustained expectancy, the medieval categorization of sin made hope's annulment, despair, one of the "deadly" sins— literally, a sin driving toward death, whether spiritual death or actual suicide. Of all the cardinal sins, despair has been considered by the hamartiological tradition the most fearful; thus in *Inferno* Dante saw written over the portals of hell, "Abandon hope, all ye who enter here." Hell in most Christian literature is eternal separation from God, ergo a sphere of unrelieved despair.

Examining the statistics of mental health, substance abuse, violence, crime, suicide, and the like pertaining even (and perhaps especially) in affluent contemporary societies, one could be tempted to resort directly to the language of despair, but that would be a mistake and a gross simplification of this profound category of Christian hamartiological tradition. Despair may *inform* destructive behavior, but it is not to be equated with the behavior as such, for it is a posture of the *psyche* (soul, mind), a spiritual condition. Destructive behavior is, in fact, usually a way of *avoiding* the truth of the soul. Very few indeed are the human beings who, despairing, have the courage, will, and imagination to face it openly, let alone give voice to it. The messages that suicidal persons leave for their relatives usually fail to name the depths of their dereliction and frequently constitute the ultimate denial of their despair by blaming their problems on others. Albert Camus, who in the twentieth century came closest, perhaps, to articulating despair, and who regarded suicide as the only truly serious philosophical question, probably did not act on his conclusions: his death was likely accidental.

But despair need not be total to be real, nor does it have to be overt. Even household dictionaries recognize this truth: "Despair: utter loss of hope, complete domination by feelings of hopelessness, futility or defeat, wildly and bitterly expressed or *quietly and pervasively dominant*."[38]

Apart from particular instances, I would argue, if despair is said to be the spiritual condition of the twenty-first century, it is the latter and not the former variety that must be stressed. It is covert and not overt despair with which we must concern ourselves.

Covert despair—repressed hopelessness—is, however, by far the more insidious of the two types. It is well able to masquerade under a guise of well-being so persuasive as to deceive the wearers of the masks themselves. It can readily sublimate itself through the pursuit of activities that seem to emanate from highly positive attitudes toward life and the future. Human beings cannot live with a conscious, unrelieved sense of the "vanity" (Koheleth) of their lives and endeavors. If their gods die, if their optimism is dashed by events, if the habit of hope languishes in them, they will likely construct bogus hopes out of thin air and sheer determination. "If the world's a wilderness, go, build houses in it!"

At one level, all thoughtful people should be very grateful for such persistent if repressive determination; without it, the world would dissolve into nihilism and chaos. Ernest Becker rightly claimed that repression is to the human what instinct is to other animals.[39] The human spirit knows, at a level deeper than conscious thought, that survival depends upon hope; therefore, incipient despair is nipped in the bud before it reaches the level of consciousness. Life must go on, and so a sustained awareness of negation *must* be subverted. Christians may even want to consider such repression a form of "common grace"!

There is, however, a fine line between "necessary," life-preserving repression and the kind of repressive posture that must lie to itself so consistently that it ends in destructive behavior more devastating than the negating realities that it fears to acknowledge. Such behavior is not necessarily or ostensibly destructive of the repressing *self*; more frequently, its victims are those round about: spouses, children, friends, coworkers, and others, whose very existence must be lashed out against because it is too transparent of the delusions the despairing subject has determined to maintain. This psychic phenomenon is famously illustrated in the lives of prominent historical figures (Nero, Caligula, Richard III, for example), and it is never very far away from the deathbeds of individuals denying the possibility of their own demise (see in particular Tolstoy's *The Death of Ivan Illych*).

The Social Applications of Covert Despair

Covert despair, the despair that relieves itself at the expense of those in its environs, is not just a condition of individuals; it pertains also to entire societies and even whole civilizations. As many, perhaps beginning with Augustine, have shown, Rome in its decline was far more destructive than it was in its ascendancy. The ravages of its rise to imperial status were inspired by a genuine (if, from a biblical point of view, demonic) expectancy: the early Caesars believed themselves to be building a humane, ordered, and civil ecumenical society. In its decay, however, Rome's idealism gave way to cynicism in the intelligentsia, and heroics to brute force and militarism. Now Rome was attempting to sustain its illusions of greatness by embracing an assumed eternality (the "divinity" of the emperor was not emphasized earlier). It strove to account for its failures by locating their cause in "the enemy," especially allegedly internal enemies. The periods of serious Christian persecution, to mention only one such "enemy," correspond with the increase of repressed anxiety—the anxiety that can be viewed still today in the sculpted faces of the patrician classes of the period. One must at least ask (and many commentators on the decline of "the West" and its successive empires *have* asked) whether this phenomenon inheres in the logic of empire.

Covert Despair as the Absence
of Operative Systems of Meaning

The anatomy of despair, particularly as it applies to societies, must seek the sources of this anxiety, not so much in positive and obvious evils and wickedness (such as terrorism, warfare, financial catastrophe) as in the absence of that which gives meaning to experience, including very negative experiences. It is in the absence of the good rather than the presence of evil that despair has its genesis. Tillich insightfully named this third anxiety "meaninglessness and despair," for it is through the loss of meaning that humankind finds itself driven to despair. Even systems of meaning that, from a Christian perspective, must be regarded as questionable can be recognized as effectual in sustaining the esprit de corps of a people as long as they are credible to many or most citizens. This could be illustrated even by the early histories of Nazi Germany or Lenin's Russia. Pervasive hopelessness sets in—whether "wildly" or "quietly"—only when a system of meaning becomes threadbare and, finally, incredible.

Just at that point, however, a new danger emerges: the forcible maintenance of "the system" (as in both Hitler's Germany and Stalin's Russia) or, more subtly, the elevation to prominence of the bureaucratic, economic, and technical accoutrements of the disappearing worldview or ideology.

It is in the latter sense, I think, that we should understand the demise of modernity. The modern vision, with its roots in the seventeenth century, its elaboration in the eighteenth-century Enlightenment, and its activation in nineteenth-century industrialism, visibly began to wind down in the latter part of the nineteenth century; its "death," many believe, was announced by the guns of August in 1914. But it is too easy to speak as if modernity is over and done with, let alone hail the postmodern epoch as its clear successor. In history, significant change takes time: the mechanism of the clock may stop, but the pendulum may continue to swing of its own momentum for a very long time!

Although the utopian dreams of modernity have failed, some of them conspicuously, the accoutrements of those dreams have by no means disappeared. They have risen, rather, to the surface, filling the vacuum left by the effective demise of the system of meaning that spawned them. By accoutrements I mean such factors as these: (1) a technicalized rationalism, rationality deprived of depth and lacking its critical dimension; (2) unchecked capitalism, capitalism minus the "invisible hand" and shorn of the philanthropic obligations felt by earlier capitalists; (3) crass and ever crasser forms of consumerism; and (4) unlimited exploitation of the natural order. Of all these, as of other tendencies that could be named, one can say that they are means no longer answerable to operative ends. The ends to which they were in some real way accountable have quietly disappeared with the system of meaning of which they were constituents.

By comparison with the present, modernity's conception of the human (*imago hominis*) must be regarded as a "high" anthropology. It was certainly anthropocentric, and theocentric religion always had a quarrel with it for that reason; yet, partly because of its Judeo-Christian antecedents, the modern vision at its height retained an image of man [*sic*] that was able, while it was operative, to reject certain conceptions of human life and to limit the expressions of human desire that seemed incompatible with that image. Again, modernity embraced what was for serious Christians an impossibly idealistic conception of the capacity of human reason—almost a deification! Yet the Enlightenment and, in a different way, the romantic movement were both able to hold technique accountable to higher dimensions of human thought. With the demise of the modern vision as a viable system of meaning, however, man was reduced to will, and reason to "technical reason" (Tillich) or "calculative thought [*rechnendes Denken*] (Heidegger); technique was no longer answerable to anything beyond its own dynamism and the whims of its high priests and beneficiaries. One could not count any longer on reason (represented by the universities, for instance) to call halt to any given project. Modernity's elevation of man, now deprived of romanticism's belief in *homo sapiens* as nature's child and preserver, was reduced to nature's master and, indeed, its sworn enemy, who would use it without reverence for his own purposes, no questions asked! It is not, finally, the limitations and failures of modernity as such that Christians should lament but the (perhaps inevitable) reduction of the modern vision to truncated versions of its own principal themes. The grave instabilities unleashed by the effective death of the modern system of meaning and the takeover of its accoutrements constitute the daily bread of our despair.

The despair as such, however, is profoundly hidden—especially from those who benefit most from the (temporary!) economic and cultural "success" made possible by means no longer answerable to just ends. To confront our despair, in such societies, requires a courage and truth orientation that few discover within themselves. It would in fact require embracing another system of meaning, an alternative vision of the good with which to fill the emptiness that is left by this ending. Only such a new system of meaning could provide the permission that is needed to name and attempt to alter the bogus goals and cheap hopes that are the residue of modern Prometheanism, for, false and unworthy as they are, those goals and hopes are all that is left of the bright visions of the architects of modernity. We fear to lose them and, besides, they are very firmly entrenched. Meaning has departed; the system remains.

The Victims of Covert Despair

Covert despair applies most directly and obviously to the materially successful peoples of our planet, peoples whose collective spiritual poverty is most conspicuous in their attempts to find meaning in materiality (consumerism, the cult of the body, the quest for status and permanence through ownership, etc.). It is, of course, a *human* response to the vulnerability of creaturehood, when people repress their deepest fears, and as such it may be found everywhere—among the have-not as well as the have peoples. But as a broad pattern of social behavior, such unacknowledged anxiety typifies the possessing more immediately than it does the dispossessed. Possession itself, including the power that attends it, cushions the shock of the abyss of meaning over which it is built. North Americans' present comforts and diversions shield them from the need to come to terms with the future that is begged by their assumed nonchalance.

It is not so with the dispossessed. To be poor, hungry, ill-clad, inadequately sheltered, or in other ways physically deprived; to be at the mercy of gross economic injustice, ethnic violence, or political chaos; to be rejected or marginalized on account of race, gender, class, ethnicity, or sexual orientation—such conditions not only leave little space for the luxury of repression but also represent an actualization here and now of the "shock" that possessing peoples are able to relegate to an indefinite future. The despair that is felt by "the rich" as an unwelcome presence at the back of their minds is for "the poor" an unavoidable reality. Paradoxically, it is perhaps just because the poor cannot avoid confrontation with the pathos of their human condition that remarkable expressions of hope are frequently found among them, thus demonstrating the biblical dialectic of hope and despair, namely, that hope, when it is authentic, arises out of the crucible of hopelessness—that it is always in some sense "hope against hope" (Rom. 4: 18).

We must distinguish, then, between the despair of the possessing peoples, which is characteristically covert, and that of the dispossessed, which is more often overt. But in the reality of planetary life today, the two despairs are complexly interwoven. Although the ultimate cause of all human anxiety must be located by Christians in the mystery that is signified by the word *sin*, at least in the realm of the penultimate it is necessary to posit a clear causative relation between the covert despair of the possessing peoples and the perennial hopelessness of the dispossessed. In their refusal, or their inability, to confront openly the reality of their hidden despair and the loss of meaning in which it is grounded, the possessing peoples of Earth perpetuate—and in their most powerful institutions *foster*!—the status quo of the two-thirds world. Despite the altruistic intentions of the have nations, despite the genuine good will and charity of many organizations (including churches) within those nations, and despite the nervous duplicity of many of us who, our rhetoric notwithstanding, participate in the prosperity of those who possess, it is as hard for the rich to achieve solidarity with the poor as it is for them to enter the kingdom of God—which, for all practical purposes, may be the same thing! And the reason for this difficulty should not be located in some vulgar accusation of mere selfishness! To make a real step toward such solidarity, the possessing peoples of the planet would have to engage in a process of *self*-knowledge that very few of us can manage, and perhaps none of us implement.

To be concrete: Bill Rees, a population ecologist at the University of British Columbia, using the best and most objective data available, has concluded that "in order to bring everyone on the planet to the same general level of consumption and well-being as the average Canadian, we would need four or five more Earths—right now!"[40] The only conclusions that can be drawn from such statistics (and the same basic data can be gleaned from many sources) are that either the present imbalance of human consumption will continue or Canadians and other overconsumers will have to lessen drastically their demands upon the planet's resources. I would suggest that this *kind* of knowledge or *pre*-knowledge has been in the public consciousness of the affluent nations of the West for a very long time, and in the past two or three decades, with the growth of ecological sensitivity, it has been nearly unavoidable. But in order to act upon it in any significant manner, ordinary citizens would have to become extraordinarily willing to examine and critique the very way of life that the entire modern experiment has conditioned them to expect, and governments, responding to such grassroots awareness, would have to be ready—readier than any Western governments have so far been!—to stand in opposition to the corporate world that never ceases to entice the citizenry of developed nations to become even more devoted to the lifestyle of consumption and acquisition. One can only conclude, in the light of events and attitudes, that the possessing peoples of the planet are prepared to see the two-thirds world sink into oblivion before they will undertake any serious examination of their own expectations and the unlikely assumptions upon which those expectations are based. Of course, this is a purely temporary posture, as gross acts of repression always are. Sooner or later (sooner, if most ecologists are right), the possessing peoples, too, will be brought up short against the limitations of earth's bounty and the seeming resilience of the natural order. Then, however, it may be too late.

The Challenge

There is, I think, no easy answer to the problem with which this type of analysis leaves us, for human despair is notoriously hard to counter—especially when it is a despair whose whole energy is concentrated upon denying its own reality! According to Christian faith, it has taken the entire wisdom and generosity of God to begin—even to begin!—to transform the soul of restless, alienated humankind. Utopian solutions, even when they are clothed in the language of the sacred, are therefore to be avoided. Hope remains hope, not "sight" (Heb. 11), and Christian hope remains hope "against hope"—against all final solutions.

Given that eschatological caveat, however, it is not so hard to discern at least the kind of *challenge* to which the foregoing reflections must lead: human despair can be obviated only by a renewal of genuine hope, and *repressed* human despair can be prepared to hope again only if it is first enabled to admit itself and to face the impossibility of the artifice by which it thinks to survive the consequences of its loss of meaning. Those who despair, if they are not given some cause to think that the admission of their despair could be a means to its overcoming, will resist the confession of it so long as their material and psychic circumstances insulate them from the cold shock of reality. To repeat, only a new system of meaning can provide the permission that repressed despair needs if it is to name and attempt to replace the bogus goals and cheap hopes that are the residue of modern Prometheanism. False and unworthy as they are, those goals and hopes are all that is left of the bright visions of the architects of modernity. We fear to lose them and, besides, they are firmly entrenched. Meaning has departed; the system remains.

The question for serious Christians is this: Can Christian faith, especially in its Protestant mode, sufficiently *extricate itself* from modernity to enucleate such an alternative system of meaning? Can the Christian movement distinguish itself from Christendom with enough imagination and daring to help humanity find a way into the future beyond the demise of the modern vision and the spent imperialism of the "Christian" West?

Chapter Fourteen

The Bible as Scripted Hope

James S. Lowry

> The revelation of Jesus Christ, which God gave him to
> show his servants. . . . Blessed is the one who reads . . . the
> words of the prophecy, and blessed are those who hear and
> who keep what is written in it.
>
> Rev. 1:1, 3

For many years, Herb Meza was pastor of the Presbyterian Church of the Pilgrims in Washington, D.C. While there, Herb, like the Church of the Pilgrims, developed the reputation, in and out of Presbyterian circles, of being something of a highly respected, if outspoken, renegade. In 1981, Herb moved from Washington to become pastor of a Presbyterian congregation in Jacksonville, Florida. When he stood before the (then) Suwannee Presbytery to be examined for reception into membership, he was asked by a grumpy old codger of unremembered age and gender, "Dr. Meza, where exactly do you stand theologically?"

One could tell by its tone that the question was as definite in antagonism as it was indefinite in scope.

Still, with no more than a moment's hesitation, in his magnificent Hispanic American accent, Herb said, "Theologically, I stand somewhere near Geneva looking toward El Salvador."

Herb, I suggest, has drawn an appropriate picture of our Reformed theological location as we move with Bible in hand into the twenty-first century, confessing hope in action. From the rich theological tradition associated with John Calvin's Geneva quickly came strong affirmation from such nearby European locales as England, Scotland, and Zürich: The holy Scriptures of the Old and New Testaments are the Word of God, the only rule of faith and obedience . . . and [later] scripture principally teach[es] what [humankind] is to believe

95

concerning God and what duty God requires of [humankind];[41] . . . we affirm and avow [scripture's] authority to be from God;[42] and We believe and confess the canonical Scriptures . . . to be the true Word of God, and to have sufficient authority of themselves.[43] These confessional statements from various European catechisms are but a few examples from our sixteenth-century non-Lutheran Reformation roots, built on strongly held views of scripture. For better and worse, they mark the theological place near which we stand as we make our missional moves into the twenty-first century. Moreover, through the missionary effort of churches in the Reformed tradition, the Reformed confessional view of scripture has spread to many places around the globe, even to those places whose non-Roman practice of Christianity predates the Reformation.[44] To be sure, *near* is a relative term describing distances that vary by case. Moreover, some of the language of the place near which we stand theologically now makes many of the faithful in the Reformed family of churches uncomfortable. Nevertheless, as we approach the twenty-first century with the Christian Bible as our primary text, it is first incumbent upon us to recognize the historical-theological place near which we stand or have recently stood.

Those rooted in the Reformed tradition have gathered and yet gather enormous *authority* from the Bible for mission. For the church of the Reformed tradition, the voice of scripture is an imperative voice that must be obeyed: "Now the LORD said to Abram, 'Go from your country . . . to the land that I will show you. I will . . . make your name great, so that you will be a blessing'";[45] "Declare his glory among the nations, his marvelous works among all the peoples";[46] "Follow me, and I will make you fish for people";[47] "[Jesus] called the twelve and began to send them out two by two, and gave them authority over the unclean spirits";[48] "You are the light of the world. A city built on a hill cannot be hid";[49] "As the Father has sent me, so I send you";[50] "Go . . . and make disciples of all nations, baptizing them in the name of the Father and of the Son and of the Holy Spirit";[51] "you will be my witnesses in Jerusalem, in all Judea and Samaria, and to the ends of the earth";[52] "it was in *Antioch* that the disciples were first called 'Christian'";[53] "Then [God] said to [Paul], 'Go, for I will send you far away to the Gentiles.'"[54] The large question of authority given by Christians to their Bible in general and as mandate for mission in particular must be dealt with shortly in greater detail. For now, it is important to note that, armed with an assumed authority of scripture, we have looked not just to El Salvador but around the globe. With that vision, in the name of the God of the Bible, we have attempted to claim the globe for the God of the Bible. Embarrassingly enough, this effort sometimes has been made with apparent cavalier disregard for the fact that the Bible itself repeatedly makes quite clear its view that the globe, "from the beginning," has belonged already to the God of the Bible.

With respect to the use of scripture, just as it is necessary to acknowledge and claim our shared theological roots, it is also incumbent on us to recognize that the history of Reformed gazing toward and claiming of the world is a history of glory and shame, of faithfulness and faithlessness, of great insight and great blindness. On the one hand, the faithful and disciplined study and teaching of scripture, coupled with proclamation in word and deed of the truth of scripture, have brought thousands from darkness into the light of Christ; that is, in many quarters, through the mission of the church around the world, good news has been preached to the poor, release has been proclaimed to the captives, sight has been restored to the blind, the oppressed have been set free, and the year of the Lord's favor has been proclaimed.[55] On the other hand, sometimes through innocent naivete, sometimes through ignorance, sometimes through malicious prejudice, some who stand "somewhere near Geneva" have used scripture to thwart the truth of God, leaving thousands in deep darkness. In the cause of proclaiming the truth of scripture, countless rich traditions have been needlessly trampled and important voices have been too long and tragically ignored. In the worst imaginable cases of abuse, less than two hundred years ago, some who once stood "somewhere near Geneva" misused scripture as justification for slavery in the southeastern United States. Similarly, until very recently, some who yet stand with us "somewhere near Geneva" misused scripture as justification for apartheid in South Africa. We must face the fact that even the rich biblical image of *leading from darkness into light* has negative connotations in some quarters of the world, where Christians have misused what we believed to be our mandate from God.[56]

Having said all that, however, one must quickly add that in some large and important measure, it is others who stand with us "somewhere near Geneva" who, with the authority of the God of Scripture, have been the apostles through whom God cast out the demons of racial hatred, cultural pride, and imperial immodesty. In doing so, we have been the agents through whom God brought healing to unspeakably deep wounds and the bearers of the truth that has set people free.

In short, historically speaking, the view from Geneva through the eyes of scripture has sometimes been as through a *prism* through which, by the mercy and leading of the Spirit of God, new light and color have been added to the spectrum of the human condition. At other times, the view of scripture from Geneva has been as through a *tunnel* that would allow no light from either God or mortal to shine on the mission to which we believe God has called and yet calls Christianity. As we approach the twenty-first century, we *must* claim with wonder and gladness the great good that has come to the world from the faithful use our tradition of mission has made of the truth of scripture through the centuries, yet we *must also* approach the twenty-first century with sincere repentance for the sins of our tradition in its abuse of scripture. Moreover, our repentance must be of the sort that not only holds great sorrow for sin but also, and far more important, makes serious resolve to move away from our errors in a radically different direction in our approach to scripture and its use in mission into the twenty-first century.

Thus said, as promised, it is now important to return to the question of the *authority of scripture*. It is, of course, far beyond the scope of this study to review the long history of the ways in which the people of God have viewed that large subject. For purposes here, it is enough to say that, at our best, we Christians, as a matter of faith, have accepted the authority of scripture as coming from God as revealed in scripture under the guidance of the Holy Spirit. To be sure, we have not always agreed on our interpretations of texts and thus have not always agreed on what the authority of God in scripture requires. Though from its beginning the Reformed tradition has insisted that it is the responsibility of Christians to interpret scripture with scripture, our interpretation of scripture has not always been peaceful. In many ways, the history of Christianity in general and of Protestantism in particular is the history of how we Christians have disagreed among ourselves on questions of the interpretation of scripture. Sometimes those disagreements have been substantive. Other times, however, they have been little more than petty and internecine bickering, in which factions in the church have used scripture and a belief in the authority of scripture as means of achieving an ecclesiopolitical upper hand. For the most part, however, particularly in the Reformed tradition, there has always been basic agreement that scripture is authoritative for the life and mission of the people of God and that the authority of scripture comes from God. That such an understanding is lacking in logic to those outside the church has seldom troubled the church in any significant way. When questioned about rational justification for our trust in the authority of scripture, we often simply argue that the experience of the church has proven that our trust has been and is well placed.

In terms of mission, until very recently the church has been able to get away with that argument not because, in itself, the argument has any merit outside the church but because for more than a millennium and a half the church has made its case for the authority of scripture by depending upon, if not calling upon, the authority of one or another empire. From Emperor Constantine onward, the mission of the church has been so bound to a national sovereignty that the mission of the church and the interests of a state could hardly be separated. From the territorial concerns of ancient Rome prior to the Reformation to similar, more recent European territorial concerns to modern American economic concerns, church mission and state interests have, until very recently, served each other well. As regards the authority of scripture, with the church's mission supported and encouraged by western imperial power, the church's insistence on the authority of scripture could go unquestioned, at least outwardly, in many corners of the globe where the church has sought to evangelize the masses.[57] This close connection between the interests of western empire and the interests of the church has caused many to wish to distinguish between *Christendom* and *Christianity*, with the former being the imperial church and the latter being the purer movement associated with the followers of Jesus Christ as that movement is separate from empire.[58] As Jesus was in the world but not of it and thus able to change the world, so his followers must heed his command to do likewise.

Now, on the threshold of the twenty-first century, with respect to authority, a remarkable shift is being felt throughout the church. As is pointed out often by the contributors to this study, the church can no longer depend on the state to support its mission. In fact, with the possible exception of pockets of resistance here and there, Christendom is dead or, at the very least, dying. Now, in most places around the globe, nation-states are either indifferent to or antagonistic toward the church and its mission. Scholars are recognizing what church folk have growingly experienced for some time; that is, the church no longer enjoys the favored position in the empire it long knew as it carried out its mission in many places around the globe. Stanley Hauerwas and William Willimon have referred to Christians as *resident aliens*;[59] that is to say, they see Christians as strangers living in their own land, which has become as a foreign land. Others, especially Walter Brueggemann,[60] have preferred to expand, and I believe improve, on that observation by using the Old Testament image of *exile* as metaphor to describe the current circumstance of Christianity after the death of Christendom. *Christians in exile* may be understood as those who, in the name of Jesus Christ, live outside and, in some instances, over against the prevailing cultural and sociopolitical norms in and under which they live. That is where Christians are increasingly finding ourselves.

All of this means that, except for isolated pockets here and there, the church can no longer depend on the interests of the state to support its mission in the world. With the loss of that support, the church can no longer depend on the authority of the state to enforce its views on the authority of scripture. Until recently, in many places around the globe, when a Christian missionary boldly said, "Listen as I proclaim and teach you the Gospel of Jesus Christ as the truth of God for you revealed in scripture," that missionary was perceived as speaking with the authority of an imposing and/or alluring empire. Such was true no matter how fervently the missionary may have really believed or pretended to believe he or she was speaking only from the self-authenticating authority of scripture. Such proclamations can no longer be made or, if they are made, there can no longer be an assumption that the proclamation carries with it the authority of empire. That being the case, the church must now revisit its texts to reshape its mission from the perspective of exile.

Surprisingly, the church in exile may take great courage and be extraordinarily hopeful as it reexamines its use of text for mission into the twenty-first century. Historically, it is precisely when the people of God have been in exile that we have been most imaginative. To that end, there are amazing signs of newly imagined hope being inspired among the Christians of our tradition. It is especially true among those who take seriously the truth of God we believe to be revealed in the texts of the Old and New Testaments. Coincidentally or providentially, as we move into the twenty-first century, the timing is right for redemptive biblical visioning. Simultaneously with, and I believe not coincidental to, the demise of Christendom, Christianity finds itself at an important (providential!) juncture. The neo-orthodox movement with its renewed emphasis on the importance of scripture has left an indelible mark on the church.[61] Although there have been and yet are abuses in form and other critical methods of biblical studies that leave the texts sterile and lifeless,[62] the truth is that various critical methods of Bible study have given us valuable tools that, when *properly* used, can help us analyze and better understand the biblical texts. Liberation theology from Central American, South American, and Caribbean nations, with its important use of scripture, has served to open the eyes of many to biblical insight that for centuries had been lost, ignored, or simply not seen. The same is true of feminist theology, African theology, and Asian theology, all of which have proponents who are speaking with fresh, strong voices in their understanding and proclamation of the truth found in both testaments of the Christian Bible. All of this, of course, is converging at a time when biblical scholarship in the pluralistic[63] postmodern world is undergoing important and exciting change wherein witness to the mission of God is seen in the voice and testimony[64] of the texts themselves.

This said, speaking as Reformed scholars and pastors addressing a seminary community with an increasingly global outlook (i.e., "standing somewhere near Geneva looking toward El Salvador" and beyond), it is important to note that there is reason to be greatly encouraged by the developments some see just now with respect to approaching the texts of the Old and New Testaments; that is, precisely at the moment when (a) Christendom is convulsing in the last of its death throes, (b) the Western Christian community is rushing headlong into exile, and (c) the thousand-headed demon despair is possessing the globe,[65] while (d) there is a parallel global groveling after the false hope promised by the two-fisted golden god of militarism and consumerism—at precisely this moment, we are hearing more and more articulate, fresh, faithful voices expressing the truth of our ancient texts. Moreover, it is from these ancient texts lately revisited that we are discovering a word for Christianity set free as contrasted to Christendom tightly bound to imperial coattails. In so doing, we are finding new energy, vision, and faithfulness for looking toward the sure promises of God from the places of our recent exile.

Key to this new vision of Christianity in the world is the renewed understanding in many quarters that the mission of God is not limited to the mission of the church. We are bold to believe and affirm that our texts of the Old and New Testaments are witness and testimony to the mission of God in the world.[66] We are also bold and humbled to believe and affirm that, through the witness and testimony of the Old and New Testaments, we see ourselves called, with the generations of the faithful before and after us, to be participants in the mission of God in the world. At the same time, like confessing that the mission of God is not limited to the mission of the church, we also quickly confess the texts given particularly to the synagogue and church are not the only texts through which God chooses to speak. We must and do stop short of saying that *for Christianity* the texts of the Old and New Testaments are no more than one canon among many canons as though, *for Christianity*, our texts have no extraordinary value in their particularity and historical significance. Still, we are anxious to hear what other texts and the voices they have influenced tell of the mission of God. The same is true of oral testimony to God other than the testimony that comes to us from our own rich oral tradition.

Having said that, the texts of the Old and New Testaments remain for us the primary testimony of the mission of God in the world through which Christianity is formed and into which we believe Christianity has been invited to participate in a particular way. In bold humility, we see within the testimony of the Old and New Testaments both the call and content of the mission of the church. From the prehistory call "to fill the earth and subdue it," to the call of Abraham and Sarah to establish the people of God, to the call of Moses to lead the people of God to the promise of God, to the call of prophets and poets for the people of God to be witness to the nations, to the call of Jesus to slow-tread the road to Jerusalem, to the call of disciples and apostles to take good news to the Gentiles, to the call of the churches in Asia Minor to see visions of a new heaven and a new earth, and countless points between in the biblical witness, we see ourselves invited and commanded, in covenant with God, to join God in God's mission to the world.

As latter-day exiles considering our use of scripture as we move with hope into the twenty-first century, we will make many important observations and discoveries. Three of those will be treated here.

First, as exiles, we may find new images for ourselves by revisiting old images from our texts that recount the activity of God in our forebears when they were in exile. We may see ourselves as Joseph quietly knowing a "bigger picture" while serving in the courts of Pharaoh.[67] We may see ourselves as wildly imaginative Ezekiel calling on the breath of God to bring new life to "these dry bones,"[68] or as Esther

becoming queen and a strong and subversive influence over Aha-
suerus, ruler over "one hundred twenty-seven provinces from India to
Ethiopia,"[69] or as Daniel and his friends remaining faithful to God
while serving in the courts of Nebuchadnezzar,[70] or as Isaiah with a
vision for exiles of the servant who is light to be the nations,[71] or as
John of Patmos with a vision for the churches of "a new heaven and a
new earth."[72] These, of course, are but a few of the biblical images of
the faithful in exile.

Second, we *must* (and there really is no option here) *invite* people
into our texts and trust the testimony of the texts to find authority from
the God to whom they bear witness; that is to say, with no claims left
to imperial power, the church should and must give up all effort to
impose our texts and the God of our texts on anyone. Happily, the narrative nature of (much of) the Bible summons just such faithful use of
the Bible. For purposes of illustration, I wish to suggest that the Gospel
of Mark is a particularly helpful case in point. Although Matthew with
"the Great Commission" as its closing verses, Luke-Acts with its
movement from the Gospel of Christ to the founding of the church
and its spread to the gentile world, and John with its emphasis on
"sending" have been the traditionally important missional texts, I want
to suggest that, methodologically speaking, Mark may be a particularly
important text for missional movement into the twenty-first century.
Mark, more than the others, is filled with resounding silences. Perhaps
the silences are the result of Mark's economy of words, his artistic form,
his method of "doing" theology, or all or some combination of these.
In any event, the silences are there. An important case in point, for
example, is Mark's version of the temptations of Christ. Following a
brief account of the baptism of Jesus and just before an account of the
beginning of the ministry of Jesus, we read:

> And the Spirit immediately drove [Jesus] out into the wilderness.
> He was in the wilderness forty days, tempted by Satan; and he
> was with the wild beasts; and the angels waited on him. (1:12–13)

There is, of course, great temptation to read detail from Matthew and
Luke into the story as we have it from Mark. Mark, however, by his
silence on the subject, invites the church to struggle with what the
temptations of Christ might have been. That, I suggest, is an important missional method in any generation but especially as we move
into the twenty-first century in the variety of our socioeconomic and

cultural contexts, each of which is ripe with alluring temptations to false hope. Into Mark's silence, Christians can and must invite all who will to engage questions of true and false hope.

Mark's most striking silence, of course, is to be found at the end of his closing verse (assuming the short ending to the canonical Gospel is Mark's ending). On the day of resurrection, according to Mark, after the disciples had a brief and dramatic encounter with the Risen Christ, who told them to go and tell Peter and the other disciples that he was risen, Mark ended the Gospel account with the following starkly troubling verse:

> So they went out and fled from the tomb, for terror and amazement had seized them; and they said nothing to anyone, for they were afraid. (16:8)

Into the silence generated in the stunned disciples (church), Mark invited the church to wonder and discover what the resurrection of Christ means. Through the church, the world, in the variety of its contexts, is also invited to wonder and discover the meaning of the church's affirmation of its belief in the resurrection of Christ. There could be no clearer expression of the church's missional responsibility as we move into the twenty-first century. With no authority except the authority of the God of scripture, our only missional option is to invite all who will join us in the texts to discover the truth of the testimony of the texts.

Third, with respect to the use of our texts in missional movement into the twenty-first century, another important consideration for latter-day exiles is biblical apocalyptic eschatology. In order to use the Bible's rich apocalyptic material as text for mission, the first order of business, of course, must be to rescue it not only from Hollywood film makers but also from the abusive clutches of Christianity's own ultraright wing. Such a rescue will be no easy feat, but for a world drowning in the despair of hopelessness, no single missional task could be more important for Christianity. The completely fruitless and useless energy given over to matching ancient apocalyptic images to contemporary events must be resoundingly renounced and utterly abandoned. Efforts to force meaning onto the apocalyptic imagination of our forebears does nothing so much as prostitute their method and meaning and leave their work tragically less than useless.

By rescuing the biblical apocalyptic imagination, however, Christianity can use the method of apocalyptic imagining to hold before the world drowning in despair a vision of hope borne on the promise of God. From Daniel in the Old Testament prophetic tradition, to Jesus of the synoptic tradition, to John of the Revelation, the purpose of apocalypse, *without exception*, is to hold before the people of God, precisely at the moment of their greatest hopelessness, a vision of hope of God. In no instance of biblical apocalypse is the apocalyptic vision to be used either to frighten people into submission or as an escape from present reality, as is often done in far too many latter-day popular misuses of our ancient texts. Quite to the contrary, the purpose of biblical apocalyptic vision is to enable the people of God and, through the people of God, to enable the world to deal constructively with the hopelessness of present reality. The task of Christianity in the twenty-first century (as in any century) is not to re-create fantastic ancient apocalyptic images and vainly attempt to impose them on twenty-first century audiences. The missional task of Christianity in the twenty-first century is to imagine with all the creativity we can muster what the hope of God looks like in the variety of our global contexts and to hold that vision before the world as a way of inviting people to be freed by ultimate hope in the promise of God so they can work faithfully against all present hopelessness and despair.

There are, of course, many other ways the texts of the Old and New Testaments may and must be used missionally as Christianity moves into the twenty-first century. These three are suggested here because they seem to be of particularly important significance and might not be immediately obvious.

To be sure, on the threshold of the twenty-first century, the church faces real danger in the use of its scripture. Just as outside the camp of the exiles there is the temptation to make technology and mammon into gods rather than servants of God, inside the camp of the exiles there are the twin temptations of rigid interpretation of the texts on the right and cavalier irreverence for the texts on the left. Nevertheless, there is, on many sides, strong evidence that we have before and around us a unique opportunity to heed and give witness to the truth of our texts as we move into the twenty-first century, being obedient to the call of God to join God in God's mission to the world. It is then a matter of first importance that the seminaries assure that the "teaching elders" they send to the church are well equipped to assure that the church knows its texts so that the church can faithfully live the truth of its texts.

Chapter Fifteen

A Common Hope
Is Always Context-Specific

Damayanthi M. A. Niles

Although the Christian missionary movement has always spoken
of the future in relation to the coming of a new heaven and a new
earth, it was more than often done on the basis of a strict historical
discontinuity between this world and the world to come. The old
earth will pass away and a new one will descend to take its place. In
the same way, converts were promised access to heaven, meaning an
otherworldly salvation. The promise of mission was presented as an
event to be fulfilled one day, "in another world." The many stories of
heaven and the future importance of "heaven" in mission activity
became the basis for Christianization over the years. In this way, the
work of God in Jesus Christ was removed from history and from this
world, here and now, to a place beyond history in another world,
called heaven.

The consensus of the Campbell scholars was that although hope is
transcendent it must be embodied and enacted in this world. In this
discussion, Dietrich Bonhoeffer is a very important conversation part-
ner. Dietrich Bonhoeffer distinguishes between the myth of redemption and the hope of redemption. The myth of redemption presents
the resurrection in a mythological way, which has real meaning only
after death. Inadvertently, such a claim allows death to draw the
boundary for Christian hope to be realized. Redemption means salvation for one's soul—from cares, distress, fears, sin, and death—but
it shows up only after the grave (death as perimeter), in another world
(called heaven), in another time (called eternity). "The difference
between the Christian hope as resurrection and the mythological
hope" states Bonhoeffer, "is that the former sends a man back to his
own life on earth in a wholly new way." A Christian has, Bonhoeffer
asserts, no "last line of escape."[73]

If Christian hope is to be this-worldly, it must be tied up with the hope for the whole creation. By its nature, the world is pluralistic. This-worldly hope seems to lie in participation in, and in the celebration of, the plurality that constitutes this world.

The modern experiment, backed by the values of the Enlightenment and the advances in science and technology, had confidence in establishing a stable world order. It was sustained by a confidence in the progress of the human being that would lead to the fulfillment of a perfect world order within the twentieth century. Yet the twentieth century turned out to be one of the most extreme centuries known to human history. It was a century that showed forth the heights of human ingenuity and triumphs of the human spirit. Yet at the same time, it was also a century of atrocious violence. We have seen the very best and the very worst of what the human being can be and do. Our march into the glorious future was deeply challenged, and our optimism that we can control and dominate the world and our destiny were severely shaken, leaving us feeling disillusioned and confused. This confusion marks the reality in which we now live, a time of disillusionment and despair caused by the failed modern experiment.

We have inherited from the processes of Christendom and modernity the wish to rearrange rationality, religion, and faith in such a way as to master a complex world under overarching systems. The cost of such systems is the silencing of plurality by excluding those things that do not fit into that process of thinking. Those who are silenced are inevitably the weak who do not have the power to exert their influence on the overarching project.

The problem is that an overarching project can never completely capture the reality of humanity, which is by its nature plural, and is always attempting to make sense of itself in relation to something that cannot be placed in a single worldview, that is, the transcendent. The project is doomed to fail, leaving its believers in despair. These believers then have two choices. They can create a new illusion of structure and hope, such as the new economic absolutism found in globalization, or they can find new hope by taking seriously the two interconnected issues, the reality of plurality and the reality of the excluded.

Hope seems to lie in the celebration of and participation in the plurality around us. Not only can we make sense of the fullness of life and of the reality that transcends it only through the breakdown of exclusive worldviews but also it is only through the recognition and acceptance of that plurality that the marginalized can have a voice.

When dealing with plurality, it is important to avoid two pitfalls. One is an overemphasis on similarity; the other is an overemphasis on difference. The discovery of similarity forges points of connectedness, but it can also do harm if it fails to recognize the uniqueness of each individual subject. Historian of religion Wendy Doniger calls it the problem of "all cats being gray in the night."[74]

The focus on the sameness of subjects fails to recognize the uniqueness of each individual subject. When comparing several subjects, there is the danger of lumping them together in one amorphous whole. An example of this is the so-called inclusivist method of comparing religion.[75] It is so focused on finding the similarities between religions that it ends up explaining away all the differences between religions and squeezing them into a single meta-religious framework of the method's own devising. When comparing oneself with a subject outside oneself, overemphasis on sameness can lead to absorbing them into one's own system of thought and dismissing them as an extension of oneself. A second example is the Hindu tendency to embrace all religions as part of itself—the "all roads lead to Rome" (or, more correctly, "Benares") syndrome. Both in the case of creating a meta-framework and in absorbing the Other into one's own framework, the Other becomes irrelevant as a subject unto itself.

Then again, focusing entirely on the difference between subjects makes it impossible to find a common ground from which the comparison can be made. This leads to the exclusivist method of dealing with theology, in which one way of thinking, being, or believing is preferenced as primary. An example of this is neo-orthodoxy's sharp separation of religion and revelation, seen in the work of, for example, Hendrik Kraemer. Kraemer defines religion as a human-made all-inclusive system that addresses the question, How do we understand and respond to God and God's world? Revelation, according to Kraemer, is God's attempt to be understood on God's own terms outside human ideas and experiences. Kraemer's nervousness concerning the inadequacy of human ideas and experiences to make sense of revelation leads him to overemphasis of the transcendent over the immanent. This causes problems. First, it allows a particular understanding of revelation to take on not only a normative but also an exclusive and comprehensive status. That understanding comes to be understood as the revelation itself, thus giving it a transcendental value it does not deserve. Ironically, the very thing that Kraemer wished most to avoid—namely, the human being rather than God becoming the key referent of revelation—comes to pass. Second, it leads to the slighting of the religions and the cultures that shape the language of a particular understanding of revelation. Only by understanding the religious and cultural vocabulary of a particular view can we truly begin to see why that particular view expresses revelation in the way it does. Then we can be open to both the strengths and the limitations of that particular understanding. Asian theologians who bought into this Kraemerian separation of religion and revelation looked upon the different religions as sources to be used to explain Christian claims. They felt free to borrow concepts from other religions to express their own theological ideas without having to take the soteriological claims of those religions seriously. This can be seen in the works of such scholars as Lynn de Silva and D. T. Niles, who use Buddhist concepts to do two things: first, to express the Christian faith in language that they assumed would communicate in a Buddhist context and, second, to open Christian theology to Buddhist concepts in order to widen our understanding of the Christian faith itself.[76]

A second example of overemphasis on difference is the overemphasis on a particular indigenous voice to the point that we romanticize it. There is a danger of becoming locked into genetically confined theological conversations, which assume that the only theology we can understand is the one we are biologically related to; hence, only women can understand and articulate feminism, only Koreans can understand and articulate *minjung* theology, and only Filipinos understand a theology of struggle. It also gives rise to a skewed discussion of true identity. What makes a person pure enough to understand and articulate a particular theology, and does the articulation of a particular theology make the person pure? What makes a person Korean enough to talk about *minjung* theology? Is it only people who talk about *minjung* who are Korean? It makes conversation across theological boundaries impossible. R. S. Sugirathrajah warns that the "unalloyed pure native roots" no longer exist.[77] The simple village farmer who has an innocent, practical spirituality is no more real than "the noble savage." Much of the world lives in multicultural societies, with television, Internet access, and teenage mutant ninja turtles. It is in such contexts that we live and in which we must find not only our identity but also the means to live with neighbors of multiple cultures, languages, and faiths. This romanticization also can lead to the failure to address the weaknesses within a particular theology. In her article "Creating Dangerous Memory," Kang Nam Soon warns against so romanticizing and idealizing some liberating aspect within a traditional culture that we fail to see the dehumanizing forces at work within it. For example, it may be easy to co-opt Asian female deities as a means of liberating us from patriarchy in Christianity, without taking seriously into consideration the function the same deities perform in fulfilling patriarchal expectations in the traditions they inhabit.[78] Feminist scholars have been tempted to look at the goddess, such as in the figure of Kali, as a powerful female archetype, without taking sufficiently into consideration the context in which such figures are used and how they have affected the situation of women in that context. Worship of the goddess in India tends to be predominantly a male enterprise, and in the case of Kali, part of a violent culture, such as the *thuggie* culture in South India. They worship the goddess as mother and dismiss mere mortal woman as unable to live up to those expectations. However, the dangerous and unpredictable creative power that is attributed to the goddess is transferred to the depiction of mortal women, so that men feel that women have to be controlled and tamed. As a result, the goddess figure, though powerful in itself, has not aided women. Rather, it has been used either to marginalize women or to control them. The invoking of the goddess figure in dealing with patriarchy in Christianity must pay attention to the way it is used in its original context. Otherwise, it has the potential to be used in a similar negative manner in the new one.

An overemphasis on either similarity or difference will not allow us to take seriously the multilayered, multifaceted reality within ourselves and around us. Comparison needs to do two things: it needs to defamiliarize that which has been taken for granted, and it needs to make us come to terms with the Other. Doniger chooses to look at the similarity between subjects in a manner that allows one to see the difference between them. All cats may indeed be gray in the night, but they are different cats! It is in this space between the subjects' similarity and difference that the comparative enterprise can thrive. The similarity provides a point of comparison, and the difference provides the stuff to be compared.

Hope is enacted in taking seriously the plurality around us. For religions to become agents of hope, they must be willing to be open to that plurality as the place where God resides and works. For this to happen, religions must renegotiate their absolutes. Indian theologian Felix Wilfred believes that, while religious traditions need to affirm their foundational texts and traditions, they must also be open to the future. They must be aware of their limitations and open to learn from other traditions, and they must also begin to look at truth from an evolutionary point of view rather than as a fixed reality. Movement toward greater truth is not an either/or movement from one fixed understanding of truth to another but a both/and way of thinking that happens when one modifies, rethinks, reshapes, and perhaps abandons what was thought to be true when one is confronted by other ways of thinking. Surely, if one is dealing with the transcendent, no tradition is sufficient to explain it.

The process in which religion, like all other features of human existence, is caught up is globalization. It is, therefore, a process that religion must come to terms with. Robert Schreiter describes globalization as the process of extension of modernity throughout the world while compressing our perception of time and space.[79] David Held and Anthony McGrew in their article "Global Transformations" describe globalization as "a widespread perception that there is a broadening, deepening, and speeding up of worldwide interconnectedness in all aspects of life, from the cultural to the criminal, the financial to the environmental. At issue appears to be a global shift, that is, a world being molded by economics and technological forces into a shared economic and political arena."[80] It involves the blurring of boundaries of the global and the local by the stretching of political, social, and economic activities over traditional frontiers; the intensification of interconnectedness because of the flows of trade, investment, finance, migration, and culture; the velocity of the diffusion of ideas, goods, information, capital, and people; and the deepening impact of all of this on the global situations and the local on it.[81]

Globalization has become the new means to master a complex world under an overarching system. It is a recasting of the need, found in Christendom and modernity, to synthesize the world under one grand narrative. This narrative leads to economic absolutism. Globalization uses the illusion of unity to force all of reality to serve its economic end. Those who cannot be fitted into the system—the powerless and the poor—are marginalized. This is all the more troubling because the powers that control the process are faceless and elusive.

An advantage of globalization is that it forces religions into closer proximity to each other, requiring them to recognize that each is one among many. When they can take that reality seriously, and work with and for each other while respecting each other's differences, they become an authentic means to begin to comprehend the fullness of human experience and that which transcends it.

However, while globalization helps place the different religions in closer proximity to each other, its purpose for doing so is not a true celebration of difference as a means to give voice to the excluded but a co-opting of those differences to present them as commodities of the economic and technological arena. This allows the individual to shop around and build the religious framework that fits his or her own needs without attention to the communal nature of religion. The power of globalization is its ability to focus on the individual in a way that blinds the individual to the detrimental effects of globalization on the human community and the creation as a whole. It pits the survival instincts and needs of the individual over against the creation. Globalization fails to see that creation cannot be fitted into a process and that the attempt to do so will in the end kill it.

The commodification of religion requires a subtle smoothing over of the heart of differences. In this manner, difference is made to look like similarity and therefore able to function in the framework of globalization. It is only in the willingness of religions to work out of their plurality, by taking their differences seriously, that they can create an alternative to that framework. In so doing, they create a space where those silenced by the economic and technological elite can have voice, and as a result religions can keep their own voice in the public arena. While globalization functions to exclude, it also generates interconnectedness, which the voices of the excluded can utilize for both networking and expressions of solidarity, wherein they may discover new signs of hope.

It is unhelpful, therefore, to attempt to demonize globalization as a process, as some tried earlier to demonize modernity, and attempt to return to a romanticized premodern past. It is likewise unwise to place false hope in the globalization process as means of access to utopia. We must discern a critical yet nuanced understanding of how it affects us and how it can be used and must be resisted for the betterment of all of creation.

Felix Wilfred, in his book *Asian Dreams and Christian Hope*,[82] outlines four areas of hope-generating praxis. First is the praxis of emptiness. At a time of the idealization of the market and the need to acquire, there is a need to readdress the religious discipline of self-emptiness and absence. Wilfred believes that religions that speak in terms of fullness—that is, that they have the primary hermeneutical key for understanding reality—can lean toward exclusion and arrogance. The idea that when one is busy claiming and holding on one is both less aware of that which is around one as well as less able to give has a long tradition in Asia and Christianity. A second hope-generating praxis is the movement away from individualism to solidarity with the excluded. The underlining idea is that all humans regain their dignity only when the dignity of those who have been excluded is restored. The third hope-generating praxis is the positive appreciation of the human. Although the sinfulness and brokenness of human nature is obvious, there is a need, at a time when the overwhelming nature of globalization ironically uses the idea of individualism to take away our sense of self-motivation and self-definition, to focus on the positive factors of being human. At a time of despair, there is a need for religions to radiate a sense of hopefulness about the goodness of being human to keep cynicism and manipulation from becoming the focusing agents of human action. The fourth hope-generating praxis is to be able to provide creative alternatives about what it means to be human so that one is not driven to conformism and resignation.

To do this, different religions need to be involved in hope-generating dialogue. This kind of dialogue is more than conversation. It is hope in action. It is the willingness to forge relationships and stand in solidarity with people across boundaries, not only because they are sacred to God but also because it is in those relationships that the essence of the One whom Christians call God is to be revealed.[83]

Such a dialogue may involve intensive conversation that seeks wisdom in dealing with concepts, settings of worship, prayer, and interpretation of scripture, but it is more. Dialogue is the communion of all of God's people with each other and with creation at large. Dialogical engagement, then, is not only a way of thinking and a source for doing theology, but also a way of life. The role of religion within this enterprise is to explore ways of becoming part of the dialogical process. In so doing, religions become agents that activate new expressions of hope that take seriously issues of plurality, the excluded, and the illusions of false hope.

Chapter Sixteen

Revolutionary Hope in the Church after Christendom

Ofelia Ortega

Rejection of the Christendom Illusion

For a definition of Christendom,[84] we shall take into consideration the relationship encompassing the terms *church*, *state*, and *civil society*.

Within Christendom, the relationship of church and civil society is mediated by the church-state relationship. Where Christendom is in place, the church seeks to safeguard its presence and expand its power in civil society, particularly by making use of the state.

For Douglas John Hall, "the decline and humiliation of Christendom in the West is, I have said, a process. It is not a matter of sudden death."[85] For him, "the phase of the Christian movement that we call Christendom (i.e., the domination of official Christianity in the western world) is coming—has to come—to an effective end, despite vestiges of Christendom that continue today and may continue for a long time."[86]

Gustavo Gutiérrez affirmed, "Christendom is not primarily a mental construct. It is, above all, indeed the longest historical experience the church has had. Hence the deep impact it has had on her life and thought. Let us not easily dismiss this mentality as extinct. It survives today implicitly or explicitly in large and important sectors of the Church."[87]

Pablo Richard[88] dated the first cycle for Christendom in Latin America from 1492 to 1808 (from the discovery of the Americas to the beginning of the independence struggles) and the second from 1808 to the 1960s.

During the first period, or colonial cycle (first colonial pact), Latin America Christendom was set up; during the second period, or neo-colonial cycle, the new Christendom was established. We could divide this second period into three stages (1808–1870, 1870–1930, and 1930–1960).

The crisis of Latin American new Christendom began with the advent of the structural crisis within the capitalist system, the crisis of Latin America–dependent capitalism, and the internal restructuring of economic, political, and ideological relationships, which started during the 1960s (leading toward a third colonial pact).

It was during the 1960s and 1970s that for the first time in the history of Latin America there was a direct contradiction between Christendom and church; one will be able to survive only if the other disappears. It was a time of a series of crises between new Christendom and the church.

It was clear in the analysis that the crisis of new Christendom did not stand outside the crisis of the international capitalism system.

In its effort to "Christianize" society, the church relies primarily on political society (specifically the state) and on those classes that have hegemony in political, social, cultural, and ideological life in a particular country.

The growing resurgence of the popular movement in Latin America starting in the 1960s had a direct impact on new Christendom because of its success in winning a significant place for itself among the middle and popular classes. The newness of the situation comes from the fact that it is the very social base of the new Christendom that has become socially and political involved. This social and political involvement of a significant number of Christians is well known.

In the meeting of the Commission of Studies of Church History in Latin America (CEHILA) in Cali, Colombia, in 1998, an Argentine sociologist, Hilario Wynarczk, professor of the National University of San Martín in Buenos Aires and a member of the Evangelical Church of Río de la Plata, did an analysis of what he called the "transformation of Christendom," in which he emphasized the influence of the pre-Christian religious attitudes in the religious revival in Latin America during the 1980s. He affirmed that the historical process of the conquest and colonization introduced evangelization through domination and military expansion. This historical process introduced a superficial Christianity. Then, there remained in the society an "Amerindian-substrata" in the religious culture, a second "substrata catholic–Amerindian," and a third "Hispanic Amerindian" that play an articulating role in the culture.

For Wynarczk, the actual expansion of evangelicals, the growth of the Pentecostal and neo-Pentecostal movements, and the charismatic renewal of Protestant and evangelical churches are a continuation of a mentality established through five centuries of colonial domination.

Politicians and military leaders who perceived in Protestantism an association with modernity raised the first challenges to the Catholic hegemonic role in Hispanic America in the nineteenth century.

Afterward, the arrival of historic Protestantism propitiated the separation of church and state. At the end of the nineteenth century, with the arrival of evangelical missionaries from Europe and the United States and the Pentecostals, a very strong connection with the popular sectors was established.

In the decade of the 1980s, the neo-Pentecostal movements were very well connected with the poorest people of Latin America.

Furthermore, the neo-Pentecostal religious attitudes, with their emphasis on healing and prosperity, exercised a great deal of influence in the charismatic and evangelical sectors that were established.

Then we have a change in the communication of values. A cultural influence from outside Latin America (Lutherans, Methodists, Baptists, Pentecostals, etc.) is transformed now into a "Creole evangelical culture" from the internal life of evangelical and charismatic sectors. This produces a change in the religious identity that searches to find responses to the actual crisis produced by the processes of globalization and neoliberal policies.

With regard to the evangelicals, we could say that their great transformation is surprising, not only in their theological reflection but also in their joint actions to participate actively in social changes.

The situation helps to develop energy for individual and collective social analysis and, as mentioned before, the search for a change in religious identity. Furthermore, there exists a bridge between the semantic Hispanic-Amerindian culture and the offering of symbolic goodness and values of the evangelical Latin American culture today.

Mission and Context

In a presentation given in 1992 at the Third General Assembly of Ecumenical Association of Third World Theologians (EATWOT) in Nairobi, Kenya, Franz J. Hinkelammert presented a paper entitled "Changes in the Relationships between Third World Countries and First World Countries."[89] Though Hinkelammert strictly addresses the crisis of socialism and its implications for the third world countries,

I think his analysis gives us some insight on the status of late capitalism and, given the latter's prevalence, on globalization.

Hinkelammert develops his analysis in three theses. His first thesis is that with the crises of socialism there has been a transformation in world capitalism. "Capitalism once again becomes wild capitalism, it no longer fears that alternatives are possible, and therefore does not want to compromise."[90]

According to Hinkelammert, capitalism today feels "it has won" and is now the sole system of governance that determines the value and place of personal, social, and other entities. This is capitalism "without a human face" and has no counterpart (socialism) to help keep it in check and accountable to humankind. Hinkelammert's second thesis is that, whereas the third world is economically necessary for the rich countries, its population is not needed. This has led to a change from "a world in which raw materials were exploited by exploiting the existing labor force to a world where its population itself has been made redundant."[91]

Indeed, this redundant population is seen as dangerous and no longer something to be exploited, especially in that technological development today is such that it cannot exploit this population. A significant shift resulting in this phenomenon is that the concept of exploitation now changes. As we know, the classic concept of exploitation refers to an available labor force, which is effectively used in production and from which is taken the product it makes. We are referring to the concept of surplus exploitation as it was developed in the Marxist tradition. "However, there now arises a situation in which the population no longer can be used for capitalist production and where there is no intention of using it, or any possibility of doing so in the future. A world emerges where to be exploited becomes a privilege."[92] This is an analysis not only of third world populations but also of all industrialized countries and, indeed, of all "global" communities.

Hinkelammert sees the possibility of the development of third world countries tied to development related to the world market, and his third thesis revolves around showing how first world countries will not accept this kind of development in third world countries and will systematically destroy any effort to realize this, especially via foreign debt.

Hinkelammert suggests that some alternative may be found in a solidarity understood not as solidarity of the proletariat but as a solidarity of the preferential option for the poor. However, he recognizes that present-day capitalism develops not only the denial of solidarity but also the very possibility of solidarity as well. In the end he says, "There only remains the resistance to lead our society to a restructuring of itself."[93]

In such a setting, is a commitment to the well-being of the physical human person possible? Can the ground for a genuine embodiment of Christ, the Gospel, be realized? Can any genuine constitutive symbol, the good news, actually occur apart from the commodified distortion of our modern, postmodern, and globalized context? What does it imply for the mission of the church in the twenty-first century? Will it be necessary today to reflect on the ethical foundations of mission for the twenty-first century?

As W. Brueggemann[94] affirmed, we are living "times of dislocation" in many of our disintegrating modern societies, very similar to the exile of the people of Israel. Times of dislocation always create a class of the marginalized, economically punishing the most vulnerable. But the Bible, on the contrary, presents this dislocation as motivation to construct a more just society. He points out that the people learned four types of truth that could take us out of despair and negation into a creative attitude:

- The church can learn they offer an opportunity for turning brutalizing loss into an act of faith that may in turn issue into positive energy (Lam. 1:2 and Ps. 137 and 79).
- It also models for us the disciplines of order and holiness, reordering, and renewing life through the intention of keeping communion with God, inviting God to come and dwell with us. It is what the priests of Leviticus call "disciplined holiness" or the sacramentality, which has to do with all life, the consciousness that here and now we are facing the demanding and assuring presence of God.
- We have to struggle to establish a sense of community, because dislocation brings the temptation of caring for ourselves in a selfish way. Keeping a public economy of compassion and justice is the way to go beyond despair.
- We also have to proclaim that God can create new social possibilities beyond "the shrunken horizons of defeat and submissive docility. . . . The movement is emotional, liturgical and imaginative: it requires forming a vision of the future free of the fearful dreams of entrenched power."

We have to fashion a vision of the future with new ways of talking and acting to express the new social possibilities of community transformation in terms of the neediest. We have to listen to the call God has made for us to reenter into the pain of the world and the possibility of renewal and salvation. Our missionary activity takes place in the framework of these times of dislocation, in which poverty, wars, unemployment, exclusion, and the like are common to all contexts.

Perhaps the most powerful "mission image" produced at the Eighth Assembly in Harare was the one proposed by the theologian Kosuke Koyama,[95] that "God is the God that runs" from the center to the periphery (Luke 15:20), thus transforming the periphery into the center. God turns the invisible into visible when he urges, "Quickly, bring out a robe—the best one—and put it on him; put a ring on his finger and sandals on his feet. And get the fatted calf" (Luke 15:22–23).

This image of a God who runs is a most suitable symbol for the vision of the kind of mission that we should undertake in the next millennium. Therefore, if we take seriously the context of mission, it means that the missionary activity has to be relevant to local institutions.

In the academic life of the Evangelical Theological Seminary in Matanzas, Cuba, where we teach, many of our students write their papers on subjects concerning contextual mission. With the aim of having appropriate interlocutors, we invite the local churches to the presentation and discussion of their theses. It is interesting to see their eagerness and enthusiasm to take part in these community theological-pastoral reflections, as well as to hear their comments. They help us have a more precise appreciation of the intellectual work carried out by our students. This relationship (seminary-theological education-local community) is indispensable to carry out our mission in our contextual situations.

Then again, if we analyze the context in which the missionary endeavor is carried on, we find it is in a "context of poverty, of savage capitalism which preaches and affirms a globalization at the service of less persons, making the search after profit, money, capital, into a God which requires sacrifices, no matter the social and human cost to be paid."[96]

Facing this reality, which implies the dislocation of everyday life for our peoples, "the theology of exile," which we referred to earlier, prompts us to preach and promote a "theology of life," which implies "the defense of life through human rights in the civil, political, social, cultural and ecological domains . . . assuming the radical option in defense of life which affirms the possibility of a full life in the material and spiritual realms, which includes the experience of aesthetic enjoyment, the development of creativity, the affirmation of the dignity of every human being."[97]

Is There a Way Out? Biblical and Strategic Options for the New Shape of the Church

The liberated slaves and peasants in the times of ancient Israel had the luck of being surrounded by weakened empires and kingdoms. They could try to develop an autonomous tribal society built on family solidarity (between 1250 and 1000 B.C.E.). Today, these types of societies and also the attempts to introduce alternatives to capitalism at a national level have been destroyed by the global capitalist market and Western imperialism. However, the churches and social movements in different nations can strategically keep up the vision of long-range alternatives linking the biblical message to the particular traditions, memories, and cultures of the people, instead of surrendering the myth of capitalism as the end of history.

Ancient Israel assimilated to the monarchic and tributary systems of the ancient Near East after 1000 B.C.E., and most Christian churches did the same after Constantine in the fourth century C.E. Then two strategic options arose within the ambiguities of an assimilated people of God: prophecy and legal reform.

The prophets, in the service of God's justice, faced two fronts. First was the political power of the king system, which, in a feudal period, included the economic and, of course, the ideological power. Second, from the eighth century B.C.E., a new economy was emerging from Greece, built on unlimited property rights, money, and debt mechanisms. So they had to face the powerful and the rich.

What Can We Learn Strategically from the Prophets?

One of the prophets who supports and inspires a new vision for the life of the churches in Cuba is Habakkuk. The developing of a "theology of the absurd" helped us to sustain and enrich the life of our people. "For there is still a vision. . . . If it seems to tarry, wait for it; it will surely come, it will not delay" (Hab. 2:3–4).

What a strange message, the one of this prophet who appears before us as placed on a high hill watching the horizon, dreaming with a hope, with a vision that seems to be so distant, so inaccessible, and so absurd! Habakkuk is a special prophet because he climbs to the heights of his profession and mission to watch the enigma of history and look for a solution in the light of God. Habakkuk is the "history watcher" that each epoch needs.

There is an impressive, challenging, and critical dialogue between God and Habakkuk. He is the prophet who "fights with God," reminding us of the fight between Jacob and the angel, of Moses' reasons in Exodus 3:4, or Jeremiah 1:4–10, of Job's struggle, and also of the beautiful story of the Canaanite woman who transforms the sense of the mission of Jesus himself (Matt. 15:21–28).

Habakkuk's question is useful for all times: How is it possible that the God of justice allows the powerful to oppress the righteous ones? Habakkuk asks difficult questions of God and receives answers that do not satisfy him completely.

God makes him see a coming future. The time has come for the end of the aggressive and tyrannical empire, because a more powerful empire is going to take its place. Is that a way out, going round and round in the same circle?

Habakkuk criticizes this possible solution and the oppressive military intervention. He is against a culture of violence to solve problems. Habakkuk complains again and with reason (1:11–17).

Against Oppressed Avarice

Habakkuk used his literary skill to comfort his people. So his book is like a play or declamatory piece, like a drama. Besides complaining with his God because of injustice, the prophet composes five "Alas" laments and puts them in the mouths of the victims: "They gather all nations for themselves, and collect all peoples as their own. Shall not everyone taunt such people and, with mocking riddles, say about them" (2:5–6).

We can listen to some of these laments; maybe they seem obsolete for us. On the first one, the oppressor has been accumulating foreign goods, obliging the weak neighbors "to contract debts" or "get into debt." He has combined the violent methods of plundering with violent means, apparently legal but certainly unfair: "Alas for you who heap up what is not your own! How long will you load yourselves with goods taken in pledge? Will not your own creditors suddenly rise, and those who make you tremble wake up? Then you will be booty for them. Because you have plundered many nations, all that survive of the peoples shall plunder you—because of human bloodshed, and violence to the earth, to cities and all who live in them" (2:6–8).

Furthermore, his "Alas" laments have given us a deep understanding of the ethical implications of our faith.

Against Earning without Scruple

The second one presents the scene of a house or palace where things that have been stolen are kept, a house built on an inaccessible height. In this house, built up by force of injustice and destruction, there appear fateful and antiphonal choirs, the stone answering to the wood, beams to the walls. The palace that was planned to be proud and magnificent will be the dwelling of disgrace, and the so-called inaccessibility will bring about the failure of life. Palace and height can be taken as a self-centeredness and as a cipher of the empire: "Alas for you who get evil gain for your houses, setting your nest on high to be safe from the reach of harm! You have devised shame for your house by cutting off many peoples; you have forfeited your life. The very stones will cry out from the wall, and the plaster will respond from the woodwork" (2:9–11).

The ethical problem of our times is not a residue of the past, which historical evolution could settle. It is not a question of underdevelopment, either. It is rather the opposite: the problem stems from the most developed countries. "A new social group concentrates in their hands all power and wealth: the group of 'symbol analysts,' who handle symbols but have no direct connection with the production of goods. This group amasses riches more than the bourgeoisie of the preceding industrial society. Inequalities have doubled in thirty years, according to data given by United Nations and the World Bank."[98]

In the first place, this new elite broke the social covenant of nation and work. They do not practice solidarity. They are locked in themselves and do not accept the ties and restrictions that solidarity would impose on them. In other words, such new elites break from even national solidarity. They enter into the world of the so-called globalization—a world that globalizes only the elites, leaving the masses outside, on the margin.

There is no national solidarity when the elites abandon the nation and live far from its problems. "The call for us is to develop 'a kenotic ecclesiology' which would help the churches to reflect on their internal life, stewardship of material resources and exercise of power."[99]

In the second place, these elites not only destroy national solidarity but also disrupt work solidarity. In the earlier industrial society, work was the principal means of socialization. It bestowed identity and value. Today, jobs have become temporary, diverse, insecure, and meaningless. Jobs are subject to the laws of the market, even though informally, to a considerable extent. Work has lost its dignity.

Third, education can no longer convey the "ethos of the community" in the practice of collective work, as used to be the case with the civilizations of antiquity. The main task for us will be to foster basic human education, which is teaching that which is useful for life. At present, this means to be able to socialize, be capable of working together. Only the practice of social life could instill the value of human relationship, the value of common life. Without the feeling of such value, building an ethic becomes impossible.

For this reason, as Konrad Raiser mentioned in his book *To Be the Church: Challenges and Hopes for the New Millennium*: "It seems urgent to return to the basic forms of conciliarity by strengthening the capacity for reciprocity, solidarity, dialogue and non-violent resolution of conflicts and reinforcing the process of sharing. The main emphasis should be on contributing to transformation on the level of systems by changing the cultural consciousness. The biblical concept of *metanoia*, in the sense of conversion or a change of heart, points in this direction. Such conversion is not a momentary act of moral decision, but a process of learning and a new way of living."[100]

A Culture against Violence

The third "Alas" is against violence, which was mentioned before. Yes, this is a call from Habakkuk to overcome violence!

The program to overcome violence created by the Central Committee of the World Council of Churches in Johannesburg, January 1994, has already stimulated movements among the member churches and groups related to the ecumenical movement around the world.

Nonviolence is a way of life and a system of personal, social, and international change based on the force of truth and the power of love to overcome evil and obtain justice and reconciliation.

It was striking to read the report of visits to churches in solidarity with women during the ecumenical decade. In the report of "living letters," we learned that "during our time with the churches, we note with sadness and anger that violence is an experience that binds women together across every region and tradition. The phenomenon is so pervasive that many women expect violence to be part of their lives and are surprised if it is not. Often, girls are brought up to expect violence, perhaps at the hands of a loved one. Almost everywhere we went, this reality was acknowledged."[101]

Against the Unjust Cruelty

"Alas for you who build a town by bloodshed, and found a city on iniquity!" (Hab. 2:12). The fourth "Alas" goes against the perverse lasciviousness that mixes with the joy of foreign humiliation. The scene, bravely drawn, gets a symbolic value to describe and condemn practices of international policy.

We constantly heard the news about the Mexican border of the U.S. territory. A "wall of contention" was built in Sonora, an electrified wall. The plan was organized to stop Mexican immigration at any cost.

In the new millennium, we need to become a church of the stranger, the church of Jesus Christ the stranger, according to Matthew 25:31–46. When churches close themselves to the strangers in their midst, when they no longer strive to be an inclusive community as a sign and foretaste for the kingdom to come, they lose their reason to be.

Against Idolatry

On the fifth "Alas," the prophet denounces once more the invalidity of the idols, the falsehood of the oracles. Is it going to teach you it is "a cast image, a teacher of lies?" (2:18).

In contrast, the prophet looks to Yahweh in his temple and asks for sacred silence for all nations: "But the LORD is in his holy temple; let all the earth keep silence before him!" (2:20).

Maybe this is the most appropriate conclusion of the prophetic message. Feel the presence of God and keep silence—silence to worship, to meditate reverently, and to bring up from the depths a supplication for history: "O LORD, I have heard of your renown, and I stand in awe, O LORD, of your work. In our own time revive it; in our own time make it known; in wrath may you remember mercy" (3:2).

"To turn to God" is inevitably, also, "a turning away from certain other things, from all the 'idols' which clamor for our allegiance today. The idols of wood and stone denounced by Isaiah (40:19–20; 44:9–20) have been supplanted by things far more persuasive and far more seductive: by systems of material and social gain which reward those who already have, at the expense of those who have not; by cultural and psychological systems which reward habits of domination rather than those of cooperation, sharing and solidarity."[102]

Conclusion of the Prophet: Write Down the Vision

Habakkuk is the prophet of faith. In God's answer, "The righteous will live by faith," it seems the whole vision is summed up, but it is the Hebrew notion of faith (*emunah*) applied to the righteous one. It is not faith according to our theological idea. It is better understood in the sense of fidelity, loyalty, and consistency in the search for justice.

The term is also used about Moses' raised hands when they remain firm (Exod. 17:12). The experience of faith should be always like the hands that are firmly raised for an eternal claim for justice. The prophet should keep himself in his guarding place at the wall's watch-tower, watching, waiting. And the vision shall come, because it will still wait for its time—God's time. And it is as if the vision would be pressing, by virtue of its own internal dynamism, toward a future accomplishment that would take place in God's determined moment (Isa. 55:10–11). But it should be written down. The message should be consecrated in big letters "so that it may be for the time to come as a witness forever" (Isa. 30:8).

The prophet ends his masterly prayer in chapter 3 opening up to hope (Hab. 3:17–19):

> Though the fig tree does not blossom
>   and no fruit is on the vines;
> though the produce of the olive fails
>   and fields yield no food;
> though the flock is cut off from the fold
>   and there is no herd in the stalls,
> yet I will rejoice in the LORD;
>   I will exult in the God of my salvation.
> GOD, the LORD, is my strength;
>   he makes my feet like the feet of a deer,
>   and makes me tread upon the heights."

There is a ghost that surrounds the world. A lie that has become truth. A lie that has become religion. It has many priests and followers. It is the ghost of the unchangeable world. What is normal for the ruling neo-liberal economic system of the world is abnormal for the prophets and for the gospel. It is a scandal—the scandal of famine, the scandal of violence, the scandal of the systematic exclusion of others.

What makes the prophetic message about the future so brilliant is precisely this: that in all the texts, directly or indirectly, there is an appeal to conversion and change.

It is precisely this call to change and conversion that "bothers." Nobody wants to die. Nobody wants to give away power. It is also hard to admit that the future has already begun. There are some people who prefer not to know that "the needy shall not always be forgotten, nor the hope of the poor perish forever" (Ps. 9:18). But for the prophets hope was a matter of principles. Not waiting, not dreaming of a better tomorrow, is one of the worst forms of incredulity.

Would it be possible to be committed with the vision that waits for us? Would it be possible to be sons and daughters of the coming tomorrow? Could hope as a principle be part of our own flesh?

It is true that there are prophecies that were never accomplished, but it is not because the vision was not real or because the prophets were mistaken. No, simply because we did not act as "history watchers," men and women of the coming tomorrow. That's why today Habakkuk calls us desperately to keep hope.

> For there is still a vision for the appointed time;
>   it speaks of the end, and does not lie.
> If it seems to tarry, wait for it;
>   it will surely come, it will not delay.
>
> (Hab. 2:3)

What Do We Learn Here about Niche Alternatives?

After 586 B.C.E., during and after the catastrophe of destruction and exile, there was a deep rethinking and search for alternatives. The priestly prophet Ezekiel made a particular contribution to the conversion and new beginning. So did the Priestly Codex, including Leviticus 25, with the Jubilee texts portraying God's Suffering Servant and a new exodus (Isa. 40–55).

The situation of diaspora and the semi-autonomous rebuilding of a Judaic community within the tributary context of the Persian Empire taught the Israelites to use niches for alternatives. These living examples in the long run even contributed to the humanization of other cultures, for example, the Sabbath, breaking the cycle of exploiting of labor and earth.

Do we use the niches in our sociopolitical-economic systems as churches and social movements in order to live out examples of alternatives?

During the times of the totalitarian Hellenistic and Roman empires after 333 B.C.E., the people of Judah developed various forms of resistance as the last option in their working for alternatives.

Strategically, the key instrument is saying no when everybody else is saying yes. Daniel 3 describes the three Judaic men who resist bowing down in front of the golden statue, the incarnation of absolute political, economic, and ideological power.

The persistence in the apocalyptic resistance literature is nurtured by keeping up the hope that the Kingdom of God with a human face will overcome the beastlike empires (Daniel 2–7).

Konrad Raiser in the phrase "opening space" expresses the need for alternatives. For him "this metaphor responds to one of the essential features of a globalized world, i.e., its closed character. For the first time in human history, the world is being experienced as a closed and inescapable interdependent system. . . . It is against this background that the metaphor of 'opening space' captures the dynamic of Christian mission in an age of globalization."[103]

What specific strategic questions arise vis-à-vis the totalitarian elements of the system?

What are the points in our financial system where we can break their absolutistic power by learning to say no?

How can we nurture hope through an alternative vision and the confidence that we shall overcome?

Jesus adds two other elements to this apocalyptic culture of resistance.

The Kingdom of God with a human face is right at hand. We can realize it in small cells of disciples. What are the small-scale alternatives Christian communities and even churches can develop with regard to the money economy?

Here the inclusive Eucharistic community is the ground nurturing the economic alternatives of the Jesus movement. While building up the cells of healing, inclusion, and an alternative lifestyle in the marginalized area of Galilee, however, Jesus is attacking the nerve points of the imperial system.

The economic center of his context is the temple. In a direct non-violent action, he drives out those merchants making money from the poor and unclean (women and lepers) by selling doves for the profit of the high priests, on the one hand, and the money-changing bankers profiting from the monetary complicity between the Roman Empire and the temple, on the other. Finally, he interrupts the sacrificial worship altogether, which is promoting the ideology that the people have to sacrifice.

Jesus' militant nonviolent strategy against the powers of oppression and exploitation includes the risk of the cross, personally and also corporately for the communities of radical discipleship. But the Jesus story also shows that this is not the end. Because he does not take the same weapons as the empire, the cross reveals him as the human one and the empire as what it is, the beast. This breaks the ideological power of the empire and finally encourages disciples to go the same way. Theologically, this is expressed as faith in the resurrection and the Holy Spirit. Later, this experience is captured in the sentence "The martyrs are the seeds of the church."

Following this "logic of the Spirit," Elsa Tamez helped us to identify some of the theological perceptions of those involved in the missionary task in the early church. In her book *The Amnesty of Grace*, she asserts that justification, properly understood, is in reality a synonym for humanization. She argues that justification has far less to do with God's forgiveness of sin than with God's affirmation of life for all human beings.

In Romans, Paul was writing to communities of Christians who supposedly had already been justified and believed in the One who raised Jesus from the dead (4:24). He was not "evangelizing" the Christians of Rome, but reminding them and clarifying theologically what had taken place in the life of those communities. The heart of the specific message that Paul directed to the present reality of the Christians at Rome is found in chapter 8. That message served to strengthen the faith and hope of those who were suffering the domination and condemnation of the empire, as well as the anguish of having to submit to a law that enslaved and excluded.

Romans 8 summarizes what has been said earlier in the letter. It begins by affirming that there is no condemnation for those who are in Christ Jesus (8:1) and concludes by affirming the absence of condemnation by God (8:33), by Christ Jesus (8:34), and by the logic of the socioeconomic system of his time (8:35–37).

The Cost of Being a Prophetic Church

The prophetic Church . . . must move forward constantly, forever dying and forever being reborn. In order to be, it must always be in a state of becoming. The prophetic church must also accept an existence which is in dramatic tension between past and future, staying and going, speaking the Word and keeping silence, being and not being. There is no prophesy without risk.[104]

On April 26, 1998, we received the news that Bishop Juan José Gerardi had been killed in Guatemala. Gerardi, the auxiliary bishop of the archdiocese of Guatemala, was a church leader who championed the rights of victims, and he ended up a victim himself.

Just two days before he was killed, he had stood in the front of the same cathedral and prophetically warned that the church's mission was a dangerous undertaking. He said, "We want to contribute to the construction of a country that must be different. That is why we are recovering the memory of the people. . . . This path has been and continues being full of risks, but the construction of the Reign of God is a risky task."

Gerardi spoke those words when he presented the final report of a church-sponsored three-year "Project to Recover the Historic Memory" entitled "Guatemala: Never Again." The report blamed the military for the bulk of the violence that reigned there for thirty-six years until the December 1996 peace accords put an end to war.

Late the night of April 26, just fifty-five hours after presenting "Guatemala: Never Again," at least one unidentified assailant surprised Gerardi as he returned home to his quarters in the church of San Sebastian, located in a gritty neighborhood in downtown Guatemala City. Gerardi was putting his car in the garage when the killer or killers surprised the seventy-five-year-old prelate and struck him fourteen times on his head with a chunk of cement.

"The bishop uncovered the truth and they could not stand it, just as they could not stand it when Jesus spoke the truth," said Rigoberto Pérez, a priest in Santa Cruz del Quiche who coordinated the "Historic Memory Project" in the diocese of El Quiche.

Guatemalan bishops and almost four hundred priests led a procession that carried Gerardi around the central plaza. They then returned to the cathedral, where the murdered bishop was buried in the crypt below the altar. Thousands of Guatemalans stood weeping, many throwing red carnations onto Gerardi's casket as church leaders carried it past. Many shouted, *"Nunca mas"* (Never again) as the bishops carried their fallen colleague around the plaza. Before they made it back to the cathedral, the sky turned gray, and it began to rain for the first time in weeks.

Short before Pope John Paul II visited Cuba, the president of our country, Fidel Castro, summoned sixty-nine leaders of Protestant churches throughout the island to a meeting in order to have a dialogue.

And so it happened that during the interchange, he turned to me and asked, "What do you teach at the Evangelical Seminary in Matanzas? What are the objectives pursued by the Institution?" Indeed, the question took me by surprise, but I reacted quickly and answered: "Comandante, our main task is to develop in our students the kind of consciousness that will enable them to exercise a critical and prophetic function within the church as well as in society."

In spite of the answer, an uneasy question has been haunting me since that day: Are we really achieving such objectives in our students? And the death of Bishop Gerardi has moved me to reflect even more upon this hard and difficult prophetic task, demanding from us to be holders and communicators of truth, without fear or constraints.

Robert J. Schreiter reminded us that

> "when we offer the cup in the Eucharist, we are making some very strong commitments. Those who preside at the Eucharist and offer the cup, presenting it to the people during the Eucharistic prayer and offering it to God in praise, must ask themselves: When we present this cup, can we stand worthily as individuals who can indeed sum up the sufferings of Christ's living body today—the church—and offer them to God? And when eucharistic ministers and believers offer and receive the cup in communion, saying 'the blood of Christ' and affirming it with Amen, they must ask themselves: Are we ready to take on the sufferings of Christ's living body? Do we have the courage to offer that cup of suffering to one another, knowing that to follow Jesus will bring us into conflict and adversity? Holding up and receiving that cup is a commitment to sharing in deepest solidarity with the victims of this world—those who undergo pain, those who must await redemption."[105]

A Mission That Inspires Hope

Jürgen Moltmann, the "theologian of hope," warns us that hopelessness is latent in the utopia of the status quo. The neo-conservative utopia about the "end of history" prescribes the cancellation of all utopias about the future, in favor of what we have at present.

It is better to rely on what we possess than to dream of futures that appear to be dangerous. Life becomes a cycle enclosed within the limits of things foreseen. One will not believe in whatever goes beyond what we already have—simply said, one will not believe. Incredulity has seized the hearts and lives of people and given rise to hopelessness. It is no wonder, then, that this utopia of the status quo is regarded as the worst of all utopias. No doubt, it can be good for those who enjoy certain privileges in life. However, it is the condemnation of those who live in misery or under the scourge of iniquity, poverty, injustice, and oppression. It is a utopia for the well-to-do people.

There is a great attraction in this neo-liberal utopia. It is the utopia of the status quo that promises the attraction of the good life—a life without problems or dread, within the world integration process (globalization). Of course, it is a life that belongs to those who may content themselves with what exists.

Three-fourths of humankind do not have a share in this expectation in the world, nor may a third of the society of the first world afford to be all too happy with the existence of the present. It is a restricted utopia—a utopia for those in a good position.

However, the attraction of the good life of the satisfied minority offered by neo-liberalism or late capitalism arouses undue expectations in the poverty-stricken people of this world. People in misery are eager to live in the way advertised on TV all over the world. It is the attraction of "to have." The American-European way of life exhibits visible glamorous signs at the shopping centers that exist in our societies.

This neo-conservative society dispenses with the biblical God and walks about visiting every sacred corner, breathing in the neo-mystical, neo-esoteric, neo-populist, neo-pagan odors. This religiosity "without God" seems to say that we cannot change reality, so let us change our inner world and adapt it to the real.

Joachim Fest equated the collapse of the eastern bloc with the "end of utopia" as early as 1991 in *The Ruined Dream: The End of the Utopian Era*. People, he concludes, will have to live without utopia.

Christians cannot follow the course of Fest. He does not do proper analysis; he therefore makes broad strokes without differentiating between the utopia of power and the utopia of justice. The latter is deeply rooted in Judaism and Christianity. "The 'utopia of justice' is more alive than ever it was: human dignity and the right to walk with head held high, universal human rights and democracy."[106]

Globalization makes it more important to retrieve the Christian roots of the utopia of justice. As globalization increases inequality among humans, threatens the social agendas of states, and reduces the dignity of millions on planet Earth, the utopia of justice becomes more important than ever before. The confession of hope is deeply rooted in Judeo-Christian notions of a utopia of justice. Justice shall reign and world shall be made more "human." These words should capture our mission in the twenty-first century. Mission movements grow out of utopias. The question is only, What *kind* of utopia?

This brief overview of utopias and counterutopias in our present society allows us to speak about a shade of utopia fading, but not its disappearance. The utopia does not disappear from society, or from the heart of human beings, as long as they breathe with a minimum of freedom and a minimum wish for liberation and salvation.

Back in 1951, the Protestant theologian Paul Tillich gave voice to his unease with obscurantist antiutopianism and in some of his writings deliberately assimilated utopia into his theology. In the essay "Critique and Justification of Utopia," Tillich established a necessary bond between immanent and transcendental utopias: "A Kingdom of God that is not involved in historical events, in utopian actualization in time, is not the Kingdom of God at all but at best only a mystical annihilation of everything that can be 'Kingdom'—namely, richness, fullness, manifoldness, individuality. And similarly, a Kingdom of God that is nothing but the historical process produces a utopia of endless progress or convulsive revolution whose catastrophic collapse eventuates in metaphysical disillusionment."[107]

In the same article, Tillich describes masterfully the characteristics of utopia. Utopia is true because it expresses the essence of the human being, the essential purpose of its existence. We have learned through our Cuban experience that this utopian emphasis should include both social and personal aspects, because it is impossible to have one without the other. A utopia defined socially loses its intrinsic truth if at the same time it does not integrate the whole person;

in the same way, it cannot be defined individually if we do not include the social aspect.

The art of healing can serve as an illustration: we cannot be healed apart from our social context, but the *social* cannot produce all the individual and personal healing that we need.

The second positive characteristic of utopia is to yield fruits. This means that utopia opens up the possibilities that seemed lost. Those cultures that are locked in without utopia are imprisoned in the present without a vision of any future.

According to Tillich, power is the third characteristic of utopias, in the sense that utopias are able to change the status quo. Judaism is perhaps the greatest utopian movement in history. It has taken humanity to another level of existence through that utopia of the Kingdom of God.

However, no utopia has power if it is exclusively economic, intellectual, or religious. All utopias should be holistic, including all these aspects. For utopias, there are possibilities and impossibilities of being realized, though, and paralyzing disappointment can result.

For this reason, when referring to utopias, we should speak, with Leonardo Boff, about long-term, middle-term, and short-term prospects. When we consider the prophetic line of the Old Testament, we can discover in the great prophets an oscillation or dialectical movement between a partial transcendence we may call utopia in the political sense and radical transcendence, which indicates the irruption of the divine breaking through this horizontal dimension.

In the prophetic texts, we find the political, social, economic, and intellectual dimensions, but at the same time the utopia goes beyond history itself, because it contains also an apocalyptic-eschatological element that transcends the world, as in the utopian vision in Isaiah 65 of a kingdom of peace, where human beings, animals, and creation form a reconciled, pacific, and harmonious unity. Therefore, mission should be sustained by hope, facing the "culture of despair" that tries to eliminate the "open horizons" for our peoples.

Is it possible to hold this "culture of hope" against the despair and agony of our societies, which undergo the assaults of unemployment and famine as a result of the economic, political, ideological, and religious system of our times?

Walter Altmann, a Brazilian Lutheran theologian, affirms: "Yes, we can and we should, because our hope is based upon:

- The testimonies of resistance and capacities for survival of all the oppressed groups, especially the indigenous populations, blacks and women.
- We celebrate our hope in our liturgies through our festive songs in our peoples, with our prayers and biblical reflections, in which the doxological and eschatological unite.
- The ultimate dignity of the human being cannot be crushed; all totalitarian governments have experienced this fact."[108]

This theological reality is expressed by the concept of the "image of God." We can pervert it totally, but we cannot annihilate it. This idea of the image of God irrupts wherever oppression seems to be most terrible, and even when whole peoples can be eliminated. The image of God remains in the memory of God. The exterminated are received in the cosmic heart of God.

As it is stated in the theological document on the theme of the Eighth World Council of Churches Assembly: "The extent of the value of our hope is given by the fact that it was born and has flourished in a face-to-face rejection of death." And I dare to add, and by the constant affirmation of life, which cancels on our part any commitment or alliance with those moved by the "logic of death," who carry out genocide wars as an essential component of their political practice.

For that reason, our sense of mission needs to be pervaded with a hope focused basically on the healing of the human community, as well as on the commission to work together, so as to turn hostility into friendship and break the spiral of violence that surrounds us today.

And then, what we in fact need is to create communities of viable life in this kind of mission, which inspires hope.

Chapter Seventeen

God's Mission Taken Up as the Mission of the Church

Janos Pasztor

When we approach a certain subject, we are influenced by our experiences. There is preunderstanding in all of us. Meditating upon the theme given in the title, one has to speak out of one's particular context. In the case of the present writer, the context is the central part of the continent of Europe, where the various trends of theological development have often been born or have been almost immediately heard and reflected upon over the years from the tenth century onward.[109] The geographical situation has been a very significant part of that context. The river Danube and the road system of ancient Rome helped the communication even before the modern development of railways, automobiles, and Internet connections.

The Reformation had radically transformed the life of the church in Hungary, and the various trends of thought of post-Reformation Europe exercised significant influence on it. The Protestant orthodoxy, followed by the "Cartesian turn,"[110] and then by the unfolding of the thoughts and events of the Enlightenment all had their impact on teaching and proclamation in the church. This period in that part of Europe, too, was characterized by the dynamic interaction of the philosophical development between Protestant orthodoxy and German pietism in its interrelatedness with British revival movements. The central thrust of the impact of the various trends of thought was anthropocentrism, in both philosophy and theology. On that foundation, the ideas formed a more or less coherent worldview in most of the churches of Central Europe. In these trends, one could detect elements of English deism, French and German romanticism, and liberalism. In the life of Hungarian theological institutions, the amalgamation of liberal-rationalist tendencies was termed "vulgar rationalism." It was characterized by a more or less silent yet definite denial of the divinity of Christ, which brought about the total collapse of

Trinitarian thinking. Teaching was reduced to the Fatherhood of God. Jesus was regarded—if spoken of at all—as a human person with great ethical qualities, but he was not in the center of theological thought. Trinitarian Christology disappeared completely. This was bound to lead to a complete loss of ecclesiology. The church was regarded as a human institution concerned with ethical and practical problems. The propagation of these ideas was not limited to lectures at theological seminaries and faculties but spread over in the life of the congregation in preaching and in liturgy: Christ disappeared almost completely from both.[111] Trinitarian thinking was eradicated.

The changes came first through the various movements of awakening in Europe from the middle of the nineteenth century. The breakthrough happened as a result of the spread of the neo-Reformation theology of Karl Barth and his circle. It was, however, slow and not complete because Central Europe lived in a continued series of crises from 1914 onward until the early 1990s. In these circumstances, theologians had to give ad hoc answers to burning issues of the day. There was not much chance for comprehensive theological research. However, the importance and significance of Trinitarian thinking were recognized. On this foundation, ecclesiology is being built, with parallel efforts in the life of congregations in preaching and liturgy. This is the task of our own days. Emphasis must be laid on the mystery of the person of Christ, along with the mystery of the church. This also means that the mission of God is to be built on a Trinitarian foundation. This background and the experiences therein influence me in my attempt at formulating my views on God's mission.[112]

Andrei Rubjev[113] painted one of the most famous icons, well known all over the world. Its title is *The Old Testament Trinity*. We see on it three angels sitting around a table within a circle that expresses their unity. They look at and reach out toward one another, symbolizing that their unity is a dynamic one full of vitality. In their midst is a bowl with a slain lamb, expressing that at the very heart of their dynamic togetherness is the sacrifice: living and—if necessary—dying for one another. "The pain of the cross determines the inner life of the triune God from eternity to eternity."[114] Looking at the painting, one has the impression of a powerful unity of stability and movement: the unchanging nature of God that is not motionlessness but movement for the others. The inner life of God the Trinity is this dialectic of eternal stability and movement. To reach out and be present for the others is love. That is why the scriptures testify not only to God loving the world. They also declare that God *is* love, as love constitutes the essence of his very being. By virtue of the fact that the context of the situation of the three angels on the painting is the Lord's visit to Abraham, it also expresses that the inner dynamics of the life of God include his stepping out of Godself and turning toward those outside.

This movement of God toward that which is not God is not a practical necessity, as if God's life were not full and perfect without this stepping out of himself. There is no necessity; there is no fate (αναγκη) that would force God to turn toward those outside. It is a part of the fullness of life, which is not in need of anything from anywhere (*aseitas Dei*). Therefore, no explanation for this movement can be—or ought to be—given: it is a mystery; it is a miracle of grace. God *is* love in the very center of his life, and he *loves* the world.[115]

Scriptures testify that the purpose of this movement of God to grant full and meaningful life to all is being carried out through human agents, of whom Jesus of Nazareth is unique from the point of view of both his person and his activity. He is the Second Person of the Trinity, the Eternal Son Incarnate, who together with the Father and the Holy Spirit, as One God reigns and is to be glorified forever. He entered history, which was brought about by himself (John 10:30). In him the Father—by the power of the Holy Sprit—revealed for humankind the mystery of his inner life: the perfect unity of the Three Persons, and the essential threeness of that dynamic unity.

The ikon of Rubjev also expresses that there is no subordination of the Three Persons. They are equal in sharing the glory due to the Godhead. They share the divine nature in common. However, the relation to the other persons carries in itself the particularity of each one of them. The Father is the source (πηγη or αρχη),[116] together with the Son and the Spirit.[117] In relation to the Son is he the Father. He—not in his existence, but in his relatedness—is defined by his fatherhood (*paternitas*) to the Son, and by his breathing (*spiratio*) to the Spirit. The peculiarity of the Son is his being eternally begotten of the Father; the Spirit's uniqueness is described as procession from the father. Thus the Father is the father of the Son and is our father through Christ.

The Latin church inserted into the Nicene-Constantinopolitan Creed after *procedit ex Patre* (proceeds from the Father) the word *Filoque* (and from the Son). The original purpose was to clarify the fullness of the divinity of the Spirit. In the course of historical events, however, particularly after the Great Schism, *Filioque* became a stumbling block. It became a means of expressing the claim for hegemony of the Western church over the East when it was in a weak position, being besieged and then conquered by the Ottoman Empire.[118] This problem has serious implications in terms of both the binding power of the decision of ecumenical councils and the theological justification of doctrines. As for the dynamics of God's turning toward the world, there the views are similar in East and West. "The sending of the divine Persons into the world is inseparable from the movement of the Son and the Holy Spirit within the inner movements of the inner life of the Trinity."[119] Each person has its characteristic role in perfect harmony with the others. Therefore, the Incarnation does not dissolve the Trinity. The perfect, dynamic unity is to remain forever.

In fact, it was an eastern theologian whose views on the nature of the inner life of the Trinity have found general acceptance in the West, particularly in the ecumenical era. His propositions have given tremendous help in reaching a deeper understanding of the essence and activities of God. St. John of Damascus (679–749), building on the best traditions of the East (Athanasius, Cappadocians), further developed the mystery of Trinity in his teaching of περιχώρησις: the interpenetration (*circumcessio*) of the divine persons.[120] This doctrine expresses even more clearly the uniqueness of the dynamic unity of God in its threefoldedness. The three divine Persons "live in one another to such extent, and dwell in one another to such extent, that they are one."[121] Thus, the divine life is perfect empathy. In their interpenetration, even the differences of relationship and action bind them together. There is a perfect movement of circulation within the divine life of the Triune God. The doctrine of περιχωρησις also makes it even more emphatic that there is no subordination within Godhead: the persons are equal. They live in one another and share the same glory. They are to be glorified together. (See 1 John 4:8b–9.)

Thus the Father in the power of the Spirit sent the Son. The perfect harmony of the Divine Persons includes the understanding that the Son himself participated in the decision making.[122] The mission of the Son—for all the reasons just mentioned—means that God is present in the history of the whole creation. He is for the world and its inhabitants.

Therefore, we have to emphasize that the mission is fundamentally God's mission, which is at work in history both within and outside the church.[123]

God's mission is carried out in three well-defined, distinct series of events, which form an organic unity. This corresponds to the nature of the unity and distinctness of the three Divine Persons: they interpenetrate one another and participate in the particular activity of one another.

1. God's self-sending begins with creation and is continued in providence. He is present in his creation by the power of the Spirit. As Jürgen Moltmann expresses this, "God creates the world and at the same time, enters into it."[124] The most intensive concentration of God's presence in the world is in and through humans, who were created after the image of God. As such, humans represent him in creation by virtue of the fact that their relationship is exceptional. Thus, God's presence in history is directly related to humans who are able to observe events, reflect on them, and make decisions concerning them. Thereby, history is launched as history in a series of events observed and reflected upon. Theoretically, looking at the events quasi from outside, one can speak of objective history regardless of their not being perceived.[125] History in a real sense is always subjective because events are observed, evaluated, and recorded. Humans who have been given thereby the possibility and responsibility of shaping history in close communion with the Creator, whose image they carry, are doing this. This activity of observing events and reflecting upon them brings about the beginning of history, which has never been left alone by the Creator.

2. The second phase of God's mission is the sending of the Son, who came with the purpose of restoring and saving creation. In a sense, the sending of the Son is a continuation of providence in a special way: the Incarnation. The Son, by virtue of being born of the Virgin Mary, became fully human without losing his divinity in Jesus of Nazareth. Thus, God identifies himself with one human person, who is true God and true human at the same time. In Jesus Christ, God's reign over history is united with a human person's responsibility in shaping the same. The indissoluble unity of his divinity and humanity also expresses the fullness of salvation because this mystery opens up the possibility to be restored and to enter into full communion with him: to participate in his life and also in his activities.

The act of God in Incarnation has created the objective possibility for this salvation. This makes the sending of the Spirit necessary to bring about the subjective possibility of the same.

3. The purpose of sending the Holy Spirit is to realize the presence of God in the world in a new way: now he identifies himself with a

people. There is a definite continuity with God's making Israel his own people (Exod. 19:5), whose sufferings he suffered (Isa. 63:9a).[126] There is, however, also discontinuity in opening the doors wide for all nations to share the same privilege. The continuity with the life and witness of Israel is also present here in relation to the task of this people. They have been called to be sent. Israel was God's witness (Isa. 43:10) in the midst of the nations. In establishing the church, the Holy Spirit constructed a community whose existence is absolutely meaningless without the twofold movement of having been called and sent. The very existence of the church is the state of being sent. The Holy Spirit, by virtue of implanting the church in Christ, created this existence. Thus, the church shares Christ's mission. This whole process is expressed in the Gospel of John (see John 20:21–22).

At this point, the question has to be asked, Who are the people addressed and sent by Christ? They are the nucleus of the people of God who came in public on the day of Pentecost. The church is spoken to here: the people of God who are charged to carry on the mission.[127]

The New Testament and, within it, especially the Corpus Paulinus, including the deutero-Pauline epistles, give us detailed description of the mystery of God's people. Relying on the rich inheritance of the Old Testament, a good number of images are given to enlighten readers about the church: the vineyard, edifice, the plowing field, flock, bride. Out of these images emerge as the most important ones the people of God and the body of Christ,[128] which are not images only, but historical and ontological realities.

One of them is the people of God. It is a fact of history denied by none, not even by the most unrelenting enemies of the chosen people of the God of Abraham and Jacob, who is the father of Jesus Christ. This people has been present in history, witnessing to God by its existence right through the ages. There have been different views and evaluations of the historical-empirical fact of Israel and the church. Their existence could not be reasonably denied.[129] This people listens to the voice of God and is involved in carrying out its mission. It is also an empirical fact that this people has not always lived according to the expectations, in various ways of disobedience.

The other biblical image of special significance is the body of which Christ is the head. This image is absolutely necessary to express the relationship of God with his people. It is not just people wandering through history and living under the leadership of God, who guides them by his Word through chosen servants of God: prophets, priests, and kings. Something more and deeper has been experienced and is spoken of in the Scriptures.

The closeness of the relationship between this people and the Lord amounts to God living in them and they living in God (Gal. 2:20). The image of the people is not enough to describe the depth of this reality. The scriptures witness to God sharing the life of his own people and them sharing the life of God. This sharing must be spoken of as organic unity, which is given within the structures of a body in which things are not lying side by side but have grown together. By calling a people, God has brought about a new reality, the church. The concept of people must be extended (stretched) to give a true account of it. Phenomenologically, the church is people who assemble together. However, they carry a mystery: they have been united with Christ in his death and are united with him in his resurrection through baptism by the power of the Spirit (Rom. 6:3–11; 8:9). This experience of dying and rising with him results in being engrafted[130] in him and living in him as parts of his body. The mystery of the body is twofold: first, the real divinity and humanity are being united in Christ. In his very life, the organic unity of the Creator and creatures is given. Second, the other side of the mystery is that Jews and Gentiles are together sharing the life in the body, living with the same promises as partakers of the same heritage of the fullness of salvation. Ephesians 3:3–6 is one of the most detailed descriptions of this mystery. According to this passage, the organic belonging together is described by three Greek words: συγκληρονομα (co-heirs); συσσωμα (body-together); συμμετοχα (co-partakers).[131] Each one of these puts a heavy emphasis on the reality of participation, which is in accordance with the setup and function of the body.

That is why Karl Barth could say that the church is the new form of existence of Christ.[132] Newbigin expressed the same reality by referring to the church as a new ontological reality, which is the very body of Christ.[133]

It is important for the clarity of our thinking to keep the right balance between the two sides of the one reality: people and body. The power of the Spirit and the Word of God will remind us that Christ is the head of the body; without him and without the activity of the Spirit, the body is dead. The context of talking about the body, along with other images of the church in scripture, must be taken seriously to prevent overemphasizing the body concept in itself.[134] If we take, for example, 1 Corinthians 10:1–14:40, it will be clear for us that the body language is absolutely necessary in talking about and taking practical steps toward the fulfillment of the church's mission. The connection with the people of the Old Testament, baptism, Eucharist, liturgy, and *diakonia* are all directly related to the new reality, the body of Christ.[135]

Thus we can sum it up as God's people, which is the mystical body of Christ with which the Lord identifies himself in order to empower them to carry on their mission.

Without the Incarnation and without the outpouring of the Holy Spirit, the fullness of mission—that is, the life of the church—would have no meaning, probably not even existence. As Annamarie Aagaard, the Danish theologian, puts it:

> The God of mission is to be witnessed to as Father, Son and Holy Spirit. . . . The proclamation of the sending of the Holy Spirit expresses the conviction that God . . . who realized his promises in Christ, is present in history, as God the Holy Spirit. . . . The two events of the mission (*i.e. = the sending of the Son and the sending of the Spirit*) are of equal significance. . . . Without the mission of the Holy Spirit the story of Christ is just an event of the past. . . . Only through the presence of the Holy Spirit . . . can the hope of life be alive. Consequently it can be affirmed that without receiving the mission of the Holy Spirit the historical character of the Christ-event is completely lost."[136]

The great creeds of the church, both Apostolic and Nicene, have followed the Trinitarian character of God's life and activities and are divided into three articles. They confess the inner economy of the Trinity: the Father's work, creation and providence; the Son's work, redemption; and that of the Holy Spirit, consecration, or making the chosen ones holy and fit for mission. Just as there is interpenetration among the Three Persons, the same is to be said of their activities. Each one of the three spheres of activity is dynamically and mutually interconnected.[137]

The continuity of mission therefore can be summed up: Father–Son–Holy Spirit/One God → Jesus Christ → Church (= the community of those engrafted in Christ by the Spirit).[138] This is a holy continuity and sharing with the life and activity of the Trinity. This κοινωνια (sharing)[139] was experienced by the early church. For them—and for many over the centuries—this participation in the life and work of God the Trinity became alive within the liturgy in the sanctuary, as well as in the liturgy of daily life.[140] This experience was later formulated as the doctrine of the Holy Trinity. They knew that in glorifying and praising God their lives were extended, enriched, and filled with meaning (Ps. 138:1–3, especially 3b). This experience and the ancient acclamation

> *Glory be to the Father and to the Son and to the Holy Spirit.*
> *As it was at the beginning, is now and ever shall be, world without end!*

preceded the formulation of doctrine.

Thus, praising the Lord (worship) and mission form an organic unity in various ways. God calls to embrace his people in sharing Christ in order to be sent out to continue doing the same. Therefore, John 20:19–23 has been regarded also as a paradigm of Christian worship: Christ the Risen One is present. He grants them his peace of God, which transcends all understanding (Phil. 4:7), brought about by his cross (Col 1:20). Lesslie Newbigin thus writes about this:

> ... the gift of peace is not for them [the disciples] alone. On the contrary he has chosen and appointed them to be bearers of shalom into the life of the world. Forty times in this Gospel Jesus is described as the one sent by the Father; now he sends them to continue and to complete his mission. This mission wholly defines the nature of the Church as a body of men and women sent into the public life of the world to be bearer of that peace which Christ has wrought by the blood of his cross. They will participate in his mission as they participate in his passion. The authentic marks of apostolicity will be the marks of tribulation (e.g. I Cor 4:9–13; II Cor. 6:3–10; 11:22–29). It will be as they carry in the body the death of Jesus that the life also of Jesus will be manifest in them (II Cor. 4:10). . . . Only the Spirit of him, who is the truth can so consecrate them. . . . The Church consecrated in the truth by the promise of the Spirit, is sent into the whole world. . . .[141]

The liturgy of the Reformed Church in Hungary expresses the same:

> The meaning of worship of the Lord's Day is thanksgiving for the cross and resurrection of Christ. It is not just remembering . . . but also a living encounter with the Risen One . . . who is

the subject of the worship. His real presence is realized in the word preached and enacted[142] in the sacrament. By the power of His Spirit he imparts the good news of victory over sin and death . . . then he makes them involved in the mission entrusted to him by the Father. . . . Now he imparts for them his Spirit who enables them to carry out their mission.[143]

Unfortunately, his experience of encountering and sharing the life and mission of Christ has been weakened and blurred in the course of the history of the church. The result has been a great variety of distortion of worship (such as the magical-superstitious concept of sacraments, or reducing it to an intellectual-moral event with the lecture of the "enlightened" rhetor-preacher). These distortions of the worship service were followed by distortions of missionary practice or disappearance of mission altogether.

It is Trinitarian theology that gives us the tools for critical examination of the ideas and practices of the church and its mission, past and present. Wherever this way of thinking prevails, creation, matter, history, and culture are taken seriously. Wherever it is missing, the way is open for all kinds of false views about the world and about the nature of the church and its mission. Trinitarian theology could have served—and in many cases it has served—to render help for critical self-examination, correction, and reconstruction of the life and mission of the church.

The formulation of the basis of Trinitarian Christology at Nicaea (325) coincided with the beginnings of the Constantinian era, which was rightly termed Constantinian-Theodosian by Douglas J. Hall.[144] This era, extending over sixteen hundred years—often called *Corpus Christianum*—was characterized by the church triumphant, ruling over all spheres of life as the only religion of the Roman Empire and its successors.[145]

It can be regarded as providential that at the time of the Nicene Council, only the first steps were taken in that direction. Constantine I (the Great) did bring the church into the power structures of the empire but maintained a balance with the traditional Roman religion and also in his relationship with the council. The Council of Nicaea could act and make decisions under the guidance of the Word and the inspiration of the Spirit. As the secular historian H. A. Drake sees it, the emperor was able "to create a stable consensus of Christians and pagans in favor of a religiously neutral public space."[146] However, this century witnessed how "the religion based on love and charity adopted the instruments of its former persecutors."[147] According to Drake's view, it cannot be attributed to one single person. The role of the bishops of the church who found themselves in a position of power cannot be denied. These struggles of the fourth century prepared the way for the decree of Theodosius I (the Great), who made the Trinity imperial doctrine (δογμα) in 381. From that time on, it was a bounden duty of the citizen to believe in and confess this doctrine. The church became the only and exclusive religion of the empire.

The application of imperial might in the life of the church resulted in manifold distortions with disastrous consequences. From that time on, the power of the empire with its military might intended to guard the unity and promote the propagation and extension of the church. It was not only the "sword of the Spirit, which is the word of God" (Eph. 6:17) that was the agent of mission and evangelism. The swords of soldiers and the skills of diplomats were added to it. The weapons used this way have proved to be double-edged. The protection and help given to the church brought with it control over its life and mission. The distortions thus developed can be summed up in the following:

1. The face of Christ enduring humiliation and suffering on the cross was transformed according to the image of the great rulers of the empire.[148] The New Testament also speaks of Christ as victorious. His lordship, however, is always kept in balance with his fulfillment of the role of the Servant of the Lord. He is the lion and the lamb at the same time (Rev. 5:5–12). "The royal banners go forward" around the cross.[149] In the Constantinian-Theodosian era, the balance is turned over: *Christus vincit, Christus regnat, Christus imperat.* Christ is the victor. The most extreme manifestations of this distortion were the Crusades. That is why it is not right to speak about crusades, even in a spiritualized-sublimated form.[150] The triumphalistic proclamation of the gospel is not biblical but Constantinian-Theodosian.

2. The coming of the Triune God in Christ through the power of the Spirit gives humans the freedom of response. In the Constantinian empire, this freedom was replaced by the threat of force or promises of imperial privileges. It is a matter of course that the person who does not give the glory to the Trinity has to die at the stake.

3. The context of the military and administrative might of the empire gave a false note, even if the gospel was purely preached. The shadow of the armed Roman soldier was behind the preacher.

4. If the mission is built upon the good will of the Emperor, or of any other earthly power—which itself has to be questioned—it is hardly the *missio Dei* any more. The scriptures demand of the state to respect the freedom of its citizens to make choices. It is desirable that the state should respect human rights, including the free proclamation of the gospel. This is the implication of Romans 13. When the state begins to proclaim a message of salvation, it is not the gospel of God the Trinity. In that case, the state gets demonized (Rev. 13). These two passages (Rom. 13 and Rev. 13) should be kept in balance. Trinitarian Christology teaches us how to do this.

5. It is clear in both testaments that the chosen people of God live among and for other people and bring God's light to them. Israel was God's witness among the nations. This is also the task of the church, to live among the people and serve them without being identical with them. They are the light (Matt. 5:14–16); they are the salt (Matt. 5:13); they are the leaven (Matt. 13:33). They are the little flock in the midst of and for the society in which they live.

6. The people who were forced or cajoled into the church brought with them their old ways of thinking about religion. For them, religion was a human affair and accomplishment, not an experience of life out of God's grace. They helped to establish in the church what was termed "justification by works."

So we can see that the greatest problem in relation to mission has been its Constantinian-Theodosian character. European Christendom regarded itself as the heir to the civilized Roman Empire over against the "barbarians." This view later was strengthened by the European development on the Enlightenment, which was the major influence on thought and practice from the seventeenth century on.[151] It also influenced the life and mission of churches. It grew together with the expansionist worldview of European culture. By that time, the theology of the church did not exercise its task in challenging certain elements of European culture contradictory to the gospel. Because of the lack of analysis of the cultural-social-political development[152] manifested in colonialism, it completely failed to assert the right of every nation to live in Christ within its own culture. The theological renewal that reasserted the significance of Trinitarian thinking gave guidance to see—in the light of the unity of creation and redemption[153]—the significance of life on the earth and in history over against the remnants of the dualistic view of reality inherited from the Hellenistic thinking prevalant in theology as well as in the secularized philosophies of the post-Enlightenment era.

The theological development of the Barthian and post-Barthian era has emphasized the absolute necessity of the critical role of theology. This is of particular significance in relation to the problems of the interaction of various cultures[154] in the life and mission of the church. This can help us to overcome the false superiority of European culture.[155]

Thus, the Trinitarian understanding of the *missio Dei* gives us the necessary help to clarify issues of missiology. What we can see today can be summed up in the following:

1. God the Trinity has been present in the world since creation and has never abandoned his handiwork. He hates nothing he created.[156] Creation and history must be taken seriously even in questions of anthropology, sociology, politics, and culture.

2. The central event of God's dealing with creation is the Christ-event, with its bearing upon the whole universe (Col. 1:15–17).

3. The significance of a Trinitarian theology of the Holy Spirit was long neglected, both for individual piety and the life of the church, which could not have come about without the creating activity of the Holy Spirit. This kind of theology gives justice to earthly life and history in such a way, which does not set apart the life of the church from the rest of creation, while keeping it in Christ. The work of the Holy Spirit makes human agency possible. "The pneumatological point of departure makes the assertion of anthropological aspect possible."[157]

4. The Trinitarian emphasis will guard against separating the Father, the Son, and the Holy Spirit from each other. This kind of separation leads to Jesulogia, Christomonism, or a kind of enthusiasm open to psychological manipulation. It is the Spirit of the Father and the Son who brings Christ into people's lives, gathers and keeps the church. Thus, the church will be the new form of existence of Christ, witnessing to the presence of God in his creation.

VENI, CREATOR SPIRITUS!

Chapter Eighteen

Communities of Hope midst Engines for Despair

Walter Brueggemann

The members of the seminar (three U.S. tax-paying citizens and five internationals) are agreed that focus on *mission* in the twenty-first century and a judgment about *despair* as context for ministry require particular attention to the present character of the United States and the unprecedented role it occupies politically, economically, militarily, and culturally in a world of developing globalization.

Vocation as Empire

The long-standing, complex "exceptionalism" of the United States has now come to fruition with enormous force and immense importance. That exceptionalism stands at the root of the history of the United States and now operates powerfully in the self-understanding of U.S. people. That exceptionalism has had, from the outset, a religious dimension, with the United States understood as an agent for God's vision of a new world; that religious dimension persists. It is nicely summed up in John Robinson's early succinct claim that the "new nation" is "a city set on a hill" (see Exod. 19:4–6; 1 Peter 2:9–10). It has, however, often been in tension with or in the service of another dimension of exceptionalism, namely, as a carrier of political and economic freedom that has come to be actualized as democratic capitalism. That vision of religious vocation, coupled with a notion of political and economic freedom, has eventuated in a growing sense of *vocation as empire*, as a force in the world capable of imposing its will and way on other parts of the world. This vocation is greatly celebrated, even while it is acknowledged with some disease, a cause for reluctance and embarrassment.

The notion of "vocation as empire" has its roots in the Monroe Doctrine that was redefined at the end of the twentieth century, when policy makers together with image makers set the United States on a course of expansionism and domination. The interplay of policy and ideology through the twentieth century has come to dramatic fruition with the fall of the Soviet Union in 1989, the emergence of the United States as "the last superpower," and an uncritical claim that we have reached "the end of history," history that culminates in the perfect hegemony of the United States, which lies beyond challenge. This political-military conviction is powerfully linked to the unanticipated globalization of the economy that has been powered by new technical competences but that was perhaps already implicitly present in the Dumbarton Oaks agreements that led to the formation of the World Bank and the International Monetary Fund. The convergence of political hegemony, military superiority, economic near-monopoly, and an ideology of exceptionalism has produced a political-economic-military-ideological force in the world that now can proceed almost unchallenged and seemingly with impunity to have its way in the world. It is largely the case that policy formation and practice, rooted in "empire as vocation," proceed without reflection upon the huge detrimental consequences of that claim for other parts of the international community and as a defining contribution to the ecological crisis.

The Gifts and Costs of Exceptionalism

This rough summary reflects in large sweep the sense of our seminar, though different members of the seminar would inevitably give a different nuance to the matter. I intend thus far that my comments should be descriptive. Four footnotes occur to me that are important for what follows:

First, although the primary force and expression of U.S. exceptionalism is, as indicated previously, military, political, and economic, *a subterranean strain of religious exceptionalism persists*. This strain on occasion serves to give uncritical force and authority to economic, political, and military matters and to turn such developments into a religious crusade. It is equally clear and important to recognize, however, that the lively religious dimension of exceptionalism also issues in a generous and pervasive commitment to humanitarian attentiveness, evoking policies, acts, and gestures that sometimes provide a ground for acute self-criticism. In important ways, it is religious exceptionalism that fosters self-criticism and larger, more generous efforts at social construction on the part of the United States.

Second, the imperial force of the United States is on occasion *a salutary force in the world*. It is the only empire, with its immense resources and political ("moral") authority, that can on occasion intervene in disputes beyond obvious "U.S. national interest" and that can on occasion impose a functioning order on contexts that might otherwise descend to savage chaos. It is possible that the force of empire in the U.S. nation-state might function as a political curb on the unfettered acquisitiveness of the economics of multinationals, though the capacity to exercise such political will is in short supply. The capacity for doing good with imperial resources is enormous and is sometimes activated by the religious exceptionalism noted before, even if that activation is characteristically with mixed motives and undertaken in self-serving ways. Among other things, the U.S. economy that lies at the center and core of the emerging global economy and that has the World Bank and International Monetary Fund as its agents in policy enactment does guarantee wealth in the world that holds the potential for enhancing the life of many lesser, albeit dependent, economies. Judged by the norms of realpolitik, one may judge U.S. imperialism as relatively benign. But judged by any critical theological standard, a more serious critique must readily be offered.

Third, the peculiar and imperialist role of the United States in emerging globalism is *of acute interest everywhere* in the world and can nowhere be a matter of indifference. For U.S. citizens, that concern is an ambiguous matter of engaging in systemic self-criticism while accepting the reality that the imperial capacity of the United States benefits its citizens, including those engaged in criticism. Conversely, the domination of the U.S. economy is of special interest to members of other economies and other nation-states, as those other economies and nation-states become increasingly defined by and dependent upon U.S. hegemony.

In our seminar, it is clear that Christians in every place and churches in every society must be concerned about the defining force and power of the United States in every sector of life and must struggle with the costs and benefits of such a defining power. Although the impact of U.S. imperialism takes many different forms and is given different nuances in different contexts, it is everywhere a defining issue for critical reflection.

Fourth, having acknowledged the sometimes salutary dimension of religious exceptionalism and having appreciated the sometimes positive impact of U.S. hegemony, our seminar has been peculiarly attentive to the *negative, destructive impact of U.S. hegemony*, both in fact and in potential. Those of us who are U.S. citizens have not come to the seminar unmindful of this urgent reality but continue to be instructed by members of the seminar from other contexts who show us in more immediate ways the character and extent of that negative, destructive impact. Part of the impact is intrinsic to the force of empire, and part of it pertains to the peculiar character of U.S. domination of the world economy.

The High Costs of Totalism

In pondering a serious critique of U.S. hegemony, it is clear to us that the object of the critique

- is not the United States as a nation-state
- is not U.S. commitment to democratic politics
- is not U.S. commitment to democratic capitalism
- is not U.S. commitment to a strong military in defense of democratic capitalism

Rather, the object of critique, in the face of negative and destructive performance, is a thin, determined ideology of the endless expansion of markets in the service of profit-driven systems that are insatiable in the accumulation of property, power, wealth, prestige, and control. This ideology, fostered and fully embraced by a powerful intentional minority, takes the form of a totalism that precludes the development of any serious, viable sociocultural force outside a profit system. That system, now operative with enormous momentum in global scope, reduces critical thinking to technical, instrumental reason, reduces social relationships to commodity exchange, and shrinks the public arena of serious communitarian meaning by reducing social virtue to private accomplishment.

The effect upon persons in the U.S. economy includes the erosion of public discourse, the evaporation of traditional social relationships, the reduction of human interaction to the exchange of goods, and the transposition of social imagination into entertainment as a narcotic litany of meaninglessness. Totalism in this ideology, rooted in a destructive exceptionalism, produces among its citizens a kind of hopelessness, an awareness (slightly hidden by commodity) that (a) one cannot succeed in commoditization because there is never enough, and (b) even if one succeeds in commoditization, it can never satisfy.

For persons and communities who seek to sustain other political economies, the mantra of "economic reform" means that the imperial monopoly of the United States will be shared with only those who submit to that ideology. The price of such submissiveness, moreover, is characteristically the loss of local and indigenous cultures and the sacrifice of social relationships that must be subordinated to profit motives. It is clear that the totalism of "economic freedom" is not characteristically democratic, for the "foreign policy" of the "global economy," rooted in the United States, is readily and easily allied with nondemocratic forces, so long as those forces accept hegemonic impact on local culture and local safety nets. As a consequence, the concentration of wealth becomes an engine for despair in societies that are helpless before the totalism rooted in U.S. exceptionalism.

Thus, at its most negative and destructive, this totalism produces twin despairs in the United States and abroad, despair hidden by "reform" for the powerful and narcotizing pop culture for the disinherited. The actual geopolitical consequences of "vocation as empire" are immensely destructive in concrete terms beyond despair. Such consequences include regular military intrusiveness with all the social costs it brings, the rape of material resources, and long-term social displacement and disorder.

A Missional Chance in the United States

This bleak picture, stated as starkly as I know how, does not nullify my earlier comment concerning salutary religious exceptionalism or the capacity of the empire to do good. This critical characterization, perhaps to be stated less savagely and starkly, clearly relates to our judgment in the seminar that despair is the defining mark of the context for church mission in the twenty-first century. This analysis poses in sharp form the question of the ways in which a community of hope may act and bear witness in response to vigorous production of despair. The question for mission is to wonder how and in what ways the scope of totalism can be broken or limited for the emergence of maintenance of human community not defined by commodity.

The problem is rendered more difficult by the fact that all of us in the seminar are in some way ambiguously situated in that totalism, benefiting even as we critique, accepting its gifts even as we consider life in a different mode. The U.S. totalism may challenge the church to greater critical obedience in relation to public life. Such obedience, which may take a variety of forms, is decisively rooted in the cross that stands as the ultimate critique of every human system and as the foundation for every God-given alternative. That obedience may take at least three strategic forms that are not mutually exclusive:

Reform. The wise, cunning, relentless effort to create will to turn political energies and economic resources toward community building. The Reformed tradition of the Christian church does not limit the notion of reform to ecclesial matters but continues to foster an engagement with the public domain (as with the "private sector") to bring every sector of life more fully under the aegis of the rule of God. It is obvious that the United States as "empire" is deeply intransigent and heavily committed to an ideology of dominance through globalization.

It is the ultimate vocation of the church to wait in hope for the end of all imperial alienation and exploitation, when

> The kingdom of the world has
>   become the kingdom
>   of our Lord
> and of his Messiah
>   (Rev. 11:15)

In the meantime, the church will urge, insist upon, and support the empire to more fully and more responsibly conform to its more generous impulses. To that end:

- The mission is to educate the church about the true situation of U.S. citizenship in an empire of enormous power and huge ambitions, to disabuse the citizenry of any "innocence" on the part of U.S. hegemony. This would include a sustained critical analysis of the ideology, propaganda, and euphemisms that give a human face to empire.
- The mission is to advocate and insist upon the more humane commitments of the United States, to identify and champion rootages that value just, peaceful, equitable orderings of power, to encourage the good—that is, to be a better empire.

(The recent campaign for third world debt cancellation is perhaps an instance of such advocacy in which the church stood among many allies.)

• The mission is to appropriate fully the force of democratic politics as a commitment quite distinct from the power and momentum of economic developmentalism and imperialism.
• The mission of the church in the United States includes strong, intentional connections with the ecumenical church in other parts of the world, especially in those societies that are the target for abuse and exploitation by U.S. imperialism—to the end that church solidarity will provide a context for alternative political-economic policies by empire.

Resistance. The wise, necessary refusal to have life organized in and defined by the pursuit of commodity, the resolve to order social relationships and community institutions for a different shared quality of life. Because the Reformed tradition characteristically has practiced positive engagement with political power, churches in the Reformed tradition—within the United States now more politically marginated—may be freshly instructed by the so-called peace churches of the Anabaptist tradition. "Resistance" is not an alternative to "reform" but may be a strategy employed alongside reform. "Resistance" may be expressed in quite visible acts of civil disobedience. But it is also possible that resistance might be the quieter, less noticed resolve to refuse participation in the extremities of imperialism. This may include the efforts to nurture congregational and family life, to disengage from the seductive power of the global economy, and to engage in less complicitous forms of economic life short of consumerism and its accompanying deceptive world of advertising that distorts God-given desires.

Alternative. The nervy imagination to organize zones of life apart from or in contrast to the threat of totalism. In more extreme measure, the mission of the church may be to disregard the institutional forms of the empire and to fashion alternative institutions of economic cooperation, health care, arts, and media in order to cultivate an environment of humanness that is not under such domination. The practice of an alternative need not directly confront or oppose the force of empire but may proceed in benign disregard and disengagement.

It is clear that *resistance* and *alternative* are not the most characteristic postures for a *Reformed* tradition that is perforce deeply public.

However, the new circumstance of now marginated and disestablished churches may indicate a reconsideration of such available strategies that the Reformed tradition may relearn and reembrace from other parts of the church.

It is clear that those who are contained and despairing cannot undertake in any sustained way *reform, resistance,* or *alternative.* Thus, the articulation and enactment of hope rooted in the gospel become a sine qua non for any serious counteraction in the world. There is no doubt that courageous, prophetic preaching and intentional imaginative liturgy are indispensable for the evocation and maintenance of a communal consciousness that makes such missional resolve possible.

Although a sketch of a hope-filled church vis-à-vis the empire can be done with some clarity, the facts on the ground are tremendously ambiguous. Nothing is gained by a disregard of that ambiguity. To succumb to the ambiguity, however, would itself be an act of despair. For that reason, it is the ongoing work of our seminar to continue to reflect as boldly and critically as we can on what we see clearly but live with deep ambiguity.

Campbell Scholars (2000)

Joanna M. Adams is pastor of Trinity Presbyterian Church in Atlanta, Georgia, and chair of the Board of Trustees of Columbia Theological Seminary.

H. Russel Botman is an ordained minister of the Uniting Reformed Church in South Africa and a professor of missiology on the Faculty of Theology at the University of Stellenbosch, South Africa.

Walter Brueggemann is the William Marcellus McPheeters Professor of Old Testament at Columbia Theological Seminary.

Douglas John Hall is emeritus professor of Christian theology on the Faculty of Religious Studies at McGill University, Montreal, Quebec, Canada.

James S. Lowry is interim pastor at First Presbyterian Church in New Bern, North Carolina.

Damayanthi M. A. Niles is assistant professor of theology at Eden Theological Seminary in St. Louis, Missouri.

Ofelia Ortega is pastor of the Presbyterian Reformed Church in Cuba and principal of the Evangelical Theological Seminary in Matanzas, Cuba.

Janos D. Pasztor is a professor of theology in Debrecen, Hungary.

Mission as Action in Hope

Our hope is in no other save in Thee;
Our faith is built upon Thy promise free;
Lord, give us peace, and make us calm and sure,
That in Thy strength we evermore endure.
                                                            (Calvin)

The three terms of this carefully articulated theme—"Mission as Action in Hope"—have as their premise our core confession of the gospel:

> The mission is *missio Dei*;
> The action is *God's action* in mending creation;
> The hope is *God's hope* for a new creation.

It is from this confession of the gospel that we may reflect upon the church's mission, a subset of the *missio Dei*. God's purpose is to bring the whole creation to well-being (*shalom*). The church, as the people of God's mission, has as its calling and purpose to witness to God's intention and to enact the power of blessing in a world beset by the threat of curse.

The theme suggests a deep and defining contrast between *action in hope* and *action in despair*. It invites reflection upon Christian hope (eschatology):

> the world from chaos to new creation;
> the people of God from weariness to glad obedience;
> the human person from death to life.

The theme invites *social analysis of the actions of despair* in every dimension of life, undertaken by the powers of despair in a world of

technique increasingly emptied of human depth and community—
actions of acquisitiveness, hate, alienation, brutality, and violence—
that reduce:

> the world to chaos;
> the people of God to paralysis;
> human persons to abandonment.

The theme invites *strategic planning* on the part of the church in
its responsibility as a counteractor of hope in every dimension of life
concerning:

> economic disparities midst God's abundance,
> political oppression midst God's justice,
> environmental exploitation midst God's fruitfulness,
> destruction of the social fabric of health, education,
>   and welfare midst God's homemaking,
> the claims of natural sciences midst the mystery of God,
> destruction of community via class, race, gender in the midst
>   of God's vision of unity,
> deep and lethal despair among those who have received
>   "everything" and whose lives yet are absent of joy.

Reflections on hope, social analysis, and strategic planning depend upon
the capacity of the people of God in mission to practice a hope that is
rooted solely in God's own hope, that must be informed by the reality of the world, but that is, in the end, unfettered by the world's fearfulness and anxiety. It is an open question whether the church can be,
or become, unfettered to face the present summons of the gospel,
given its careless, long-standing enmeshment in the fearfulness and
anxiety of the world.

Notes

1. Reflections on the relationship between Barmen and Belhar have been ongoing. Nico Horn's "From Barmen to Belhar and Kairos" in C. Villa-Vicencio, *On Reading Karl Barth in South Africa* (Grand Rapids: Eerdmans, 1988), 105–120; and his "Die Barmen Verklaring'n Belydenisskrif?" in D. J. Smit, *Teolgie-Belydenis-Politiek: Referate, response en besprekings van die Domatologiese Werksgemeenskap van SA* (1984), 34–66 are among them. There are other scholars who prefer to speak of three clauses with a preamble and a conclusion.
2. My early experience of the Presbyterian church was in the Presbyterian Church in the United States. Since the 1983 reunion of the major Presbyterian bodies in the United States, my experience has been in the Presbyterian Church (U.S.A.).
3. Enrique Dussel, *The Church in Latin America, 1492–1992* (Maryknoll, N.Y.: Orbis, 1992), 419–425.
4. Hungary was liberated by a united European army (1686) led by the Hapsburgs, who became the quasi-colonial rulers of the land for 150 years.
5. On August 20, 2000, Hungary celebrated the event of recognition by the Pope. The Ecumenical Patriarch of Constantinople was present and declared that Stephen I of Hungary was recognized as a saint by the Orthodox church, too. This event was evaluated by the secular press as an important sign of rapprochement between East and West. During the Communist years, the Reformed Church in Hungary initiated a series of dialogues with the Russian Orthodox church. After the collapse of the Soviet empire, the Patriarch of Moscow came to Budapest to thank the RCH for offering an important lifeline of communication with the world church.
6. The banknotes had the name and amount of the denominations in about twenty languages.
7. The area given to Romania was larger than Hungary itself. The Reformed church lost more than half of its congregations to the neighboring countries. The punishment character of the 1920 peace dictates can clearly be demonstrated by the following facts: the churches were cut off from the mother church in Hungary and had to organize their life apart from it. At the same time, the Serbian and Romanian Orthodox churches could remain and have remained in one organization with their mother churches. Even today, there are full Serbian and Romanian Orthodox dioceses in Hungary under the leadership of their respective patriarchs in Belgrade and Bucharest.
8. That is why Czechoslovakia and Yugoslavia both broke up after the collapse of

dictatorships. Their aim today is to be united with one another within the rest of Europe.

9. For example, the Czech Amos Jan Komensky (Comenius) and the Hungarian Stephanus Kiss de Szeged.

10. Janos D. Pasztor, "The Theology of the Serving Church and the Theology of Diaconia in the Protestant Churches and the Consequences in Hungary during the Time of Socialism" *Religion in Eastern Europe* 15 (6), (1995), 22–35.

11. *Brief Statement of Faith* (PCUSA), in *Book of Confessions: Study Edition* (Louisville: Geneva Press, 1999), 341–342.

12. "Great Prayer of Thanksgiving," in *Book of Common Worship: Pastoral Edition* (Louisville: Westminster John Knox Press, 1993), 335–339.

13. Dwight Currie, *How We Behave at the Feast* (New York and London: HarperCollins World, 2000), 20.

14. Saint Augustine, *The Confessions*, trans. Henry Chadwick (Oxford: Oxford University Press, 1991).

15. *Brief Statement of Faith* (PCUSA).

16. Thomas Thangaraj, Smyth Lecture at Columbia Theological Seminary, fall 2000.

17. Jürgen Moltmann, *The Spirit of Life* (Minneapolis: Fortress Press, 1992), 7.

18. Robert Shaw, Lectures at Memorial Church, Harvard University (1981) and Trinity Presbyterian Church, Atlanta (1982).

19. Karl Barth, *Church Dogmatics* IV.3.2 (Edinburgh: T. & T. Clark, 1962), 941.

20. George Stroup, "The Spirit of Pluralism," in *Many Voices, One God*, ed. Walter Brueggemann and George Stroup (Louisville: Westminster John Knox Press, 1998), 174, 176.

21. Shirley C. Guthrie Jr., *Christian Doctrine* (Richmond, Va.: John Knox Press, 1968), 287–288.

22. Eldrine Villafane, as quoted by H. Russel Botman, "Turning the Tide of the City: An Ecumenical Vision of Hope," address to the Ecumenical Conference of Churches, Dutch Reformed Centre, Cape Town, South Africa.

23. See Walter Brueggemann's contribution to this volume.

24. Douglas John Hall reflects on this question elsewhere in this volume.

25. Paul G. Hiebert suggests that one of the shifts that will have to be made for mission in the twenty-first century is away "from a stress on the church and the world, to God and God's Kingdom." Cf. his "Missiological Education for a Global Era," in J. Dudley Woodberry et al. (eds.), *Missiological Education for the 21st Century: The Book, the Circle and the Sandals* (New York: Orbis, 1996), 39–40. This shift, he says, will assist mission to move away from the Enlightenment thought that has dominated it for so long. The Enlightenment thinking brought the central focus on evangelization, which later developed into the idea that evangelization is only possible with church planting (Henry Venn, Rufus Anderson, Roland Allen, and Donald McGavran). Both these developments brought an obsession with the church and the world. The latter was seen as "the unreached" that are to be evangelized.

26. Although the Greek word *apokalypsis* primarily means to reveal what was hidden and can be understood as making known the secret will of God, an eschatological interpretation sends one off seeking for actions of God in our times and places. Only God can help us see these actions, through the Holy Spirit. The Spirit guides all people in God's mission with prophetic vision to see beyond the effects of nature.

27. David J. Bosch, *Transforming Mission: Paradigm Shifts in Theology of Mission* (Mary-knoll, N.Y.: Orbis, 1991), 501, points out that nineteenth-century theology has closed the book on the eschatology. Even as late as the year 1910, there was no reference to eschatology in the World Missionary Conference. Mission was then primarily understood as Christianizing and civilizing of nations via church planting. This missionary enterprise was in itself interpreted in terms of an understanding that the world organically grows towards maturity.

28. Ibid., 499.

29. Ibid., 506. I have indicated how the notion of the "orders of creation," especially as expressed in a distorted Kuyperian theology, has dominated South African apartheid theology. See *A Testimony on the Decisions of the Dutch Reformed Church* (WARC Publication 25; Geneva: World Alliance of Reformed Churches, 1994), 42–47; and "'Black' and Reformed and 'Dutch' and Reformed in South Africa," in Ron Wells (ed.), *Keeping the Faith* (Grand Rapids: Eerdmans, 1997).

30. David Bosch makes this argument under the heading "Mission as Action in Hope" in *Transforming Mission*, 498–510.

31. Donald H. Juel has argued this point convincingly in many places, most recently in "Christian Hope and the Denial of Death: Encountering New Testament Eschatology," in John Polkinghorne and Michael Welker (eds.), *Theology for the Twenty-First Century: The End of the World and the Ends of God* (Harrisburg, Pa.: Trinity, 2000), 171–183.

32. Polkinghorne and Welker, *Theology for the Twenty-First Century*.

33. Cf. Walter Brueggemann, *Hopeful Imagination: Prophetic Voices in Exile* (Philadelphia: Fortress, 1986).

34. Damayanthi Niles writes comprehensively about the meaning of this-worldly mission elsewhere in this volume.

35. "South" here no longer refers to specific geographical centers; it is used primarily as a description of social location everywhere in the world of the global economy.

36. Raimon Panikkar, *Christian Century*, August 16–23, 2000, 836; my emphasis.

37. Miroslav Volf (commenting on Andrew Delbanco's *The Real American Dream*), *Christian Century*, August 16–23, 2000, 837.

38. *Webster's Third International Dictionary* (Springfield, Mass.: Merriam-Webster, 1966); my emphasis.

39. Ernest Becker, *The Denial of Death* (Gloucester, Mass.: Peter Smith Publishing, 1998).

40. David Suzuki and Holly Dressel, *From Naked Ape to Superspecies* (Toronto: Stoddart, 1999), 42.

41. *Westminster Larger Catechism*, A.3 and A.5., in *Book of Confessions: Study Edition* (Louisville: Geneva Press, 1999), 249.

42. *Scots Confession*, Chapter XIX, "The Authority of the Scriptures," ibid., 42–43.

43. *The Second Helvetic Confession*, Chapter I, "Of the Holy Scripture Being the True Word of God," ibid., 93–94.

44. Smyth Lectures, Columbia Theological Seminary, October 2000.

45. Genesis 12:1–2.

46. Psalm 96:3.

47. Matthew 4:19.

48. Mark 6:7.

49. Matthew 5:14.
50. John 20:21.
51. Matthew 28:19.
52. Acts 1:8b.
53. Acts 11:26b (emphasis added).
54. Acts 22:21.
55. Adapted from Luke 4:18.
56. My thanks to Damayanthi M. A. Niles for making this observation in critiquing an early version of this section.
57. Konrad Raiser has a helpful treatment of these and other related themes in *To Be the Church: Challenges and Hopes for a New Millennium* (Geneva: WCC Publications, 1997). See especially chapter 3.
58. See especially the work of Ofelia Ortega elsewhere in this project.
59. *Resident Aliens: Life in the Christian Colony* (Nashville: Abingdon, 1989).
60. See especially *Cadences of Home: Preaching among Exiles* (Louisville: Westminster John Knox Press, 1997).
61. See especially Douglas John Hall's extremely helpful *Remembered Voices: Reclaiming the Legacy of "Neo-Orthodoxy"* (Louisville: Westminster John Knox Press, 1998), in which he recounts, among many other related matters of importance, the central place of scripture in the work of Barth, Tillich, both Niebuhrs, Bonhoeffer, Brunner, and de Dietrich.
62. Note especially the work of the Jesus Seminar and the countervailing work of Luke Timothy Johnson, *The Real Jesus: The Misguided Quest for the Historical Jesus and the Truth of the Traditional Gospels* (San Fransisco: Harper, 1996).
63. See especially the contribution of Damayanthi M. A. Niles to this project.
64. See especially Walter Brueggemann's major work, *Theology of the Old Testament, Testimony, Dispute, Advocacy* (Minneapolis: Fortress, 1997).
65. See especially the contribution of Douglas John Hall to this project.
66. See especially the contribution of Janos Pasztor to this study.
67. Genesis 41–47.
68. Ezekiel 37:1ff.
69. Esther 1:1.
70. Daniel.
71. Isaiah 41:1ff.
72. Revelation 21:1.
73. Dietrich Bonhoeffer, *Letters and Papers from Prison* (enlarged ed.; New York: Macmillan, 1971), 336–337.
74. Wendy Doniger, "Myths and Methods in the Dark," *The Journal of Religion* 76, no. 4 (October 1996): 531–547.
75. John Hick's work is an example of this method.
76. D. T. Niles, *Buddhism and the Claims of Christ* (Richmond, Va.: John Knox Press, 1946), 21; Lynn de Silva, "Non-Christian Religion and God's Plan for Salvation," *The Bulletin of the Study Centre of Religion and Society* 11 (April 1967): 18.
77. R. S. Sugirathrajah, "Postcolonialism and Indian Christian Theology," to be published in *Studies in World Christianity*.
78. Kang Nam Soon, "Creating Dangerous Memory: Challenges for Asian and Korean Feminist Theology," *Ecumenical Review* 47, no. 1 (1995): 29.

79. Robert Schreiter, *The New Catholicity: Theology between the Global and the Local* (New York: Orbis, 1997), 4.

80. David Held and Anthony McGrew, "Global Transformations: Politics, Economics and Culture," *ReVision* 22, no. 2 (fall 1999), 7.

81. Ibid.

82. Felix Wilfred, *Asian Dreams and Christian Hope: At the Dawn of the New Millennium* (Delhi: ISPCK, 2000).

83. See Janos Pasztor's discussion on Trinity in this volume.

84. I am using this phrase that Hans Hoekendijk used in the Domman Lectures, entitled "Horizons of Hope," at the Candler School of Theology, Emory University, Atlanta, Georgia, January 1970. According to Hoekendijk, "There may be, here and there, some Christendom pockets left."

85. Douglas John Hall, *The End of Christendom and the Future of Christianity* (Harrisburg, Pa.: Trinity, 1997), 3.

86. Ibid., 35.

87. Gustavo Gutiérrez, *A Theology of Liberation* (Maryknoll, N.Y.: Orbis, 1973), 54.

88. Pablo Richard, *Death of Christendoms, Birth of the Church*, (Maryknoll, N.Y.: Orbis, 1987), 35–36.

89. Franz J. Hinkelammert, "Changes in the Relationships between Third World Countries and First World Countries," in K. C. Abraham and Bernardette Mbuy-Beya (eds.), *Spirituality of the Third World: A Cry for Life* (Maryknoll, N.Y.: Orbis, 1994).

90. Ibid., 14.

91. Ibid.

92. Ibid., 12.

93. Ibid., 18.

94. W. Brueggemann, "Conversations among Exiles," *Christian Century*, (July 2–9, 1997): 630.

95. Kosuke Koyama, "The Happiness of Hope" (plenary presentation at World Council of Churches Harare Assembly, December 1998, photocopy material), 97.

96. W. Brueggemann, "Conversations," 630.

97. Ibid., 631.

98. José Comblin, "The Society of Wisdom and the Responsibilities of the New Wisdom Elites," *Reflection and Liberation* (Santiago de Chile) 28–31 (1996), insert.

99. Tom Best, "Turn to God—Rejoice in Hope," *Ecumenical Review* 48, no. 33 (1996): 8.

100. Konrad Raiser, *To Be the Church: Challenges and Hopes for the New Millenium*, Risk Books Series, (Geneva: World Council of Churches, 1997), 36.

101. *Living Letters: A Report of Visits to the Churches during the Ecumenical Decade— Churches in Solidarity with Women* (Geneva: World Council of Churches, 1997), 25.

102. Tom Best, "Turn to God," 6–7.

103. Konrad Raiser, "Opening Space for a Culture of Dialog and Solidarity," *International Review of Mission* 88, no. 350 (1999): 201.

104. Pablo Freire, "Education, Liberation and the Church," *Study Encounter* 9, no. 1 (1973): 13–14.

105. Robert J. Schreiter, *In Water and in Blood* (New York: Crossroad, 1988), 59–60.

106. Jürgen Moltmann, "What Has Happened to Our Utopias?" in Richard Bauckham (ed.), *God Will Be All in All: The Eschatology of Jürgen Moltmann* (Edinburg: T. & T. Clarke, 1999), 120.

107. Paul Tillich, "Critique and Justification of Utopia," in Frank E. Manuel (ed.), *Utopia and Utopian Thought* (Boston: Houghton Mifflin, 1966), 308.

108. Walter Altmann, "An Attempt to Summarize," *Ministerial Formation* 59 (October 1992): 51–57.

109. As early as 1521, Luther's teaching was proclaimed in the parish church of the Burgh of Buda and also in another places in the country. This was continued over the centuries right up until today.

110. René Descartes put the thinking person into the center of European philosophy. Philosophy ceased to be maidservant of theology. Instead of theo-centeredness, thinking became anthropocentric. Cf. Helmut Thielicke, *The Christian Faith*, vol. 1, trans. G. W. Bromiley (Grand Rapids: Eerdmans, 1974), 40–47.

111. In the Debrecen School of Theology, a seminar was held in the mid-1980s in which ten students analyzed the sermons of the great preachers of one hundred years ago. The name of Jesus was mentioned in only one of the fifty. In the nineteenth century, all ancient Trinitarian texts, which were approved by the Reformation and were used in liturgy for centuries, along with the Nicene Constantinopolitan Creed, were left disposed of.

112. It is not suggested here that the critical times belong to the past. Even the collapse of the Soviet empire did not result in life without serious struggles. There are many serious problems, even in the land where the changes have not so far been accompanied by dramatic events like those in Romania ten years ago or in Yugoslavia recently. Still, it is possible now to deal with the problems openly within our own circles, just as in the community of churches worldwide.

113. This Russian monk (1360–1430) was a very famous Russian icon painter. He regarded icon painting as the proclamation of the gospel in the tradition of St. Chrysostom, according to whom the icons were the Bible of the illiterate. He is said to have prayed and studied the scripture before painting, just like a preacher, in the course of his preparation..

114. Jürgen Moltmann, *The Trinity and the Kingdom: The Doctrine of God*, trans. Margaret Kohl (San Francisco: Harper & Row, 1981), 161.

115. Dealing with the problem of the life of Trinity in himself and toward the world, Moltmann comes to the conclusion that the traditional distinction between immanent and economic Trinity has to be surrendered. God is in himself the same as he is toward creation. He sees an interaction "between the substance and revelation, the 'inwardness' and 'outwardness' of the triune God," which works in both ways: ". . . the surrender of the Son for us on the Cross has a retroactive effect on the Father and causes infinite pain. . . . From the foundation of the world, the *opera Trinitatis ad extra* correspond to the *passions Trinitatis ad intra.* " " Ibid., 160. The latter has been expounded in details in another book by Moltmann: *The Crucified God: The Cross of Christ as the Foundation and Criticism of Christian Theology* (London: SCM; New York: Harper & Row, 1974).

116. Thomas F. Torrance (ed.), *Theological Dialogue between Orthodox and Reformed Churches*, vol. 1 (Edinburgh: Scottish Academic Press, 1985), 130.

117. Thomas F. Torrance, "The Triunity of God," in Karoly Toth (ed.), *Debrecen V: Theological Dialogue between Orthodox and Reformed Churches, Budapest, August 31– September 1987* (Budapest: Ref. Egyhazkerulet, 1987), 88.

118. The problem is twofold: 1. The Eastern church is not willing to recognize any change in the creed formulated by an ecumenical council that was carried out by lower church courts such as synods of the Latin church (Toledo), even when they were claimed to be ecumenical councils by the Bishop of Rome (Florence, 1438–1445). 2. Jürgen Moltmann—and others—are right in expressing their views that further study and discussion are necessary after the withdrawal of the *filioque* clause. Cf. Moltmann, *The Trinity and the Kingdom*, 178–187. Before such an act on the side of the Western church, the preconditions for such discussions are not given. Certain bodies of the churches in the west have shown willingness. The appendix of the *Second Helvetic Confession* (*Confessio Helveti Superior*)—one of the two fundamental subordinate standards of the Reformed Churches of the Continent of Europe—gave the text of the creed without the *filioque*. However, it was used in the liturgies of churches whose subordinate standard this confession is. Moltmann (187) proposes the formula: "The Holy Spirit proceeds from the Father of the Son, and who receives his form from the Father and the Son."

119. Annamarie Aagaard, "Missio Dei in Katolischer Sicht," *Evangelische Theologie* 34 (1974–75), 421. This concept of mission was present already in medieval Scholastic theology. Cf. Dietrich Ritschl and Werner Usdorf, *Oekumenische Theologie Missionswissenschaft* (Stuttgart: W. Kohlhammer, 1994), 113.

120. Otto Weber, *Grundlagen der Dogmatik* (Neukirchen: Erziehungsverein, 1955), 432; William J. Hill, *The Three-Personed God* (Washington D.C.: Catholic University Press), 272–274.

121. Moltmann, *The Trinity and the Kingdom*, 175.

122. As the Orthodox Reformed dogmatics put it: "Within the Covenant for Salvation (Council for Peace) of the Trinity, the Son shared in the decision of his own sending." See W. Heyns, *Reformatus Dogmatika* (Budapest: Holland-Magyar Reformatus Bizottsag, 1925), 67–69.

123. So Bishop Birkeli of the Church of Norway. Cf. Aagaard, "Missio Dei in Katolischer Sicht," 421; and "Statement on the Missionary Calling of the Church International Missionary Council, Willington 1952," in Michael Kinnamon and Brian E. Cope, *Anthology of Key Texts and Voices* (Geneva: World Council of Churches; Grand Rapids: Eerdmans, 1997), 339.

124. Jürgen Moltmann, *God in Creation* (San Francisco: Harper & Row, 1985), 15.

125. In his comprehensive study, Hendrikus Berkhof writes: "History is the study of man's actions and decisions." This sentence implies the indispensability of observation. However, its scope is narrowed down to human actions. The dynamics of the whole of creation have been left out of consideration in this important study. Hendrikus Berkhof, *Christ the Meaning of History* (Richmond, Va.: John Knox Press, 1966), 17.

126. ". . . [T]hat available, visible daily practice, constituted and undertaken humanly, interprets the defining linkages between Yahweh and Israel." Walter Brueggemann, *Theology of the Old Testament Testimony, Dispute, Advocacy* (Minneapolis: Fortress, 1997), 576. Cf. 567–578.

127. The text implies the authority given to the apostles, but should not be limited to this. All disciples are addressed, those present and the later ones. R. C. V. H. Lenski, *The Interpretation of St. John's Gospel* (Minneapolis: Augsburg, 1961), 1378.

128. Hans Kung, *The Church* (London: Burns & Oates, 1967), 203–262; Ernst Käsemann, "Unity and Multiplicity in the New Testament Doctrine of the Church," in *New Testament Questions of Today* (Philadelphia: Fortress, 1969).

129. It was interesting in the antireligious writings published in great numbers by the Communist party. They brought together a large collection of documents about the sins of the church. However, they never denied its existence. Cf. Karl Kautsky, *The Foundations of Christianity* (New York: S. A. Russel, 1953).

130. In Calvin's language, being engrafted is a significant term for baptism. *Institutio Religionis Christanae* IV.15.1.

131. It has more recently been pointed out how significant the reality of participation is in Pauline theology. Cf. E. P. Sanders, *Paul and Palestinian Judaism* (Philadelphia: Fortress, 1977), 463–472. ". . . why are you called a Christian? Because through faith **I share in Christ and then in his atonement**," question and answer 32 of *The Heidelberg Catechism* (Philadelphia: United Church Press, 1967), 38.

132. Karl Barth, *Die kirchliche Dogmatik IV/1* (Zollikon-Zürich: Evangelischer Verlag, 1953), 738.

133. Bonhoeffer emphasized that the body of Christ concept is not a metaphor but reality. See Dietrich Bonhoeffer, *Christology* (London: Collins, 1966), 59.

134. Douglas J. Hall pointed out rightly that that was the case with the *Mystici corporis Christi* of Pius XII. See Hall, *Confessing the Faith: Christian Theology in a North American Contex* (Minneapolis: Fortress, 1998), 56–59. The concept of the church as "the extension of incarnation" is different from the expression used by Barth: *Existenzform Christi*. With the latter, the reference is to Christ the head, who identifies himself with his people as his body.

135. If we follow the example of Karl Barth or Lesslie Newbigin, we shall experience this clarifying and guarding role of the texts of scripture.

136. Annamarie Aagaard, "Missiones Dei," in Vilmos Vajta, *Das Evangelium und die Zweideutigkeit der Kirche* (Göttingen: Vandenhoeck & Ruprecht, 1973), 101.

137. Thus, we can pray and sing: Come Creator Spirit. It is not just *communicatio idiomatum*, but also that of action.

138. That is why the Acts of the Apostles has often been called the Acts of the Holy Spirit or the Acts of Christ. (Cf. Acts 1:1, "Jesus began." The assumption is that he is now continuing his work.

139. The other important word expressing participation: the various forms of μετεχειν (Heb. 3:14a; Eph. 3:6, etc.).

140. Cf. the excellent book by Metropolitan Paulos Mar Gregorios, *The Meaning of Diakonia* (Geneva: World Council of Churches, 1989).

141. Lesslie Newbigin, *The Light Has Come: An Exposition of the Fourth Gospel* (Grand Rapids: Eerdmans, 1982), 268f.

142. I have proposed in several writings—unfortunately, all in Hungarian—that the traditional terminology denoting the sacraments as visible word is not sufficient and even misleading, with its reminiscences of the Platonic degrading of visible things over against invisible ones. The important thing about the Eucharist is not that it is visible. This term refers to the old Roman Catholic rule, according to which every believer must see the elevation at least on Sunday. It is not necessary to take part in it. They even had the services without communion for the adoration of the consecrated elements. The essential thing about the Eucharist is that **we do it**: we break

the bread, lift the cup, and consume the elements. In doing so, we proclaim the death of the Lord. Thus, the important thing about the sacrament that it is done: not only *verbum visibile* but also *verbum actum* (enacted word) carried out by the congregation. Thus, the Eucharist expresses the most significant point about mission: it is the activity of the whole people of God, having been authorized and sent by God himself. "The Eucharist is an acted sermon, and an acted proclamation." Archibald Robertson and Alfred Plummer, *A Critical and Exegetical Commentary on the First Epistle of St. Paul to the Corinthians*, ICC (Edinburgh: T. & T. Clark, 1958), 249.

143. *Istentiszteleti Rendtartas a Magyarorszagi Reformatus Egyhaz szamara [Book of Common Order in the Reformed Church in Hungary]* (Budapest: MORE Sajtoosztaly, 1985), 30–31.

144. Hall, *Confessing the Faith*, 104.

145. The control of the church has never been complete. The situation from this point of view was different in east and west. Furthermore, secularization—getting certain areas out of ecclesiastical control—began already with the Renaissance and is coming to an end in our days.

146. H. A. Drake, *Constantine and the Bishops:The Politics of Intolerance* (Baltimore: Johns Hopkins University Press, 2000), xv. This remarkable book, written by a secular historian, goes into lengthy detail to follow the very complex dynamics of the events of the state-church relationship during the fourth century. He comes to the conclusion that it was not just Emperor Theodosius I (the Great) who decided to make and uphold Christianity as the only official religion of the empire. The bishops contributed a great deal toward this development.

147. Ibid., 10.

148. Jürgen Moltmann, *The Crucified God* (San Francisco: Harper and Row, 1974), 236.

149. *Vexilla Regis prodeunt*, "The Royal Banners Forward Go." The famous hymn of *Venantius Fortunatus of Poitiers* expresses beautifully this truth.

150. Writing from prison, Dietrich Bonhoeffer raised his voice against this in *Ethics* (New York: Macmillan, 1965), 356.

151. The Enlightenment claimed to have brought light after the "darkness" of the Middle Ages and regarded the white race as carrier of the light to all parts of the world. That is why the French Revolution helped French colonial expansion. The qualitative superiority of the white race was an integral part of the self-consciousness of the European colonialists. The same thinking and attitude characterized most of the mission work: the white man is the chosen race who takes the light to the darkness of the "natives." Among the various extremities, such as the treatment of Indians in the Americas, the most extreme formulation was that of the ideology behind the apartheid formulated by Reformed so-called theologians. Thorough analysis of that attitude and practice was a result the theological renewal of the twentieth century. The latter, however, inherited ways and methods of analysis from the development of secular historical research. This development has given examples of the significance of interaction between theology and other branches of sciences, humanistic or technological.

152. Trinitarian thinking makes the analysis of the cultural, political, and economic contexts with all means available and/or the use of such analyses binding for theologians. In earlier missionary practices, such analyses were lacking. Missionaries were

often not trained for that. However, in spite of human weaknesses, the gospel was the power of God in many situations (Rom. 1:16).

153. That is why already the early eucharistic prayers offered thanksgiving for both creation and redemption. It was necessary in their struggle against gnostic dualism. Even during the centuries when dualism prevailed or at least lurked, the eucharistic prayers reasserted the significance of life on earth and Christian responsibility for it.

154. Thomas Thangaraj of Madurai, professor at Emory University, addressed this question from the point of view of an Indian Christian in his Smythe Lecture at Columbia Theological Seminary, October 11, 2000.

155. The significance of Paul's proclamation of Christ in non-Jewish culture can be found in Acts 14:8–18; 17:16–34). According to the report of Luke, in Lystra and Athens Paul was involved in a dialogue with representatives of the local culture and proclaimed the gospel accordingly, using their language. In Europe even today, one can hear opinions according to which these particular speeches of St. Paul were formulated and delivered in "disobedience."

156. "Almighty and Everlasting God, you hate nothing you have made," in the Lenten prayer (Ash Wednesday), *Book of Common Prayer*.

157. Rudolf Bohren, *Predigtlehre* (Munich: Chr. Kaiser, 1964), 74.

Index

sports and entertainment, ideology, 55
St. Augustine, 164 n.14
St. John Chrysostom, 168 n.113
St. John of Damascus, 140
St. Thomas, 43
Stephen I of Hungary, 163 n.5
stewardship, 21
Stroup, George, 64, 164 n.20
Sugirathrajah, R.S., 166 n.77
survival, depends on hope, 86
Suzuki, David, 165 n.40
syncretism, fear of, 42
Szeged, Stephanus Kiss de, 164 n.9

Taglaferri, Mario, 48
Tamez, Elsa, 129
Thaangaraj, Thomas, 61, 164 n.16, 172
    n.154
Theodosius, 147
theological education, 21
    eurocentrism, 20
theology, and identity, 110
    feminist, 111
    of the absurd, 121
    Trinitarian, 138
Tillich, Paul, 83f, 88, 133f, 166 n.61, 168
    n.107
Tolstoy, Leo, 87
Torrance, Thomas F., 168 n.116, n.117
totalism, 55
    ambiguity as critique, 156
    effects, 154
Trinity, and the economy of mission, 144

dynamic unity, 140
triumphalism, 14, 21, 53, 67, 147, 149
truth, evolutionary view, 112
Tutu, Desmond, 75

United States, as last superpower, 19f
    domination of culture, 35
    economic imperialism, 8
    exceptionalism, 151f, 154
    imperialism, 153
    self criticism, 153
universities, corporate takeover, 56
utopia, neoconservative vision, 132ff
    visions of, 88

Venn, Henry, 164 n.25
victimization, psychology of, 43
Villafane, Eldrine, 164 n.22
Villa-Vicencio, C., 163 n.1
virtual reality, 55
Volf, Miroslav, 85, 165 n.37

Weber, Otto, 169 n.120
Welker, Michael, 165 n.31, n.32
Wilfred, Felix, 111, 113, 167 n.82
Willimon, William, 100
World Alliance of Reformed Churches,
    32
World War I, peace treaties, 52
worship, relation to mission, 145f
Wynarczk, Hilario, 116

Zacchi, César, 46, 48